The
BEST
WORDS

Other Books by Robert Hartwell Fiske

The Dictionary of Concise Writing

The Dimwit's Dictionary

The Dictionary of Disagreeable English

Silence, Language, & Society

101 Wordy Phrases

101 Elegant Paragraphs

Vocabula Bound 1: Outbursts, Insights, Explanations, and Oddities (editor)

Vocabula Bound 2: Our Wresting, Writhing Tongue (editor)

The
BEST
WORDS

ROBERT HARTWELL FISKE

Marion Street Press

Portland, Oregon

A Note on Pronunciation

The syllable shown in all-capital letters signifies principal stress; the syllable or syllables shown in italics signify secondary stress; for example, the pronunciation of *amanuensis* is shown (ah-*man*-yoo-EN-sis), principal stress is on EN, secondary stress is on *man*.

Published by Marion Street Press
4207 SE Woodstock Blvd # 168
Portland, OR 97206-6267
USA

http://www.marionstreetpress.com/

Orders and review copies: (800) 888-4741

Printed in the United States of America

ISBN 978-1-933338-82-8

Cover art direction by Nicky Ip
Author photo © 2011 Susan Hedman

Library of Congress Cataloging-in-Publication Data

Fiske, Robert Hartwell.
  The best words : more than 200 of the most excellent, most desirable, most suitable, most satisfying words / Robert Hartwell Fiske.
      p. cm.
  Includes index.
  ISBN 978-1-933338-82-8 (pbk.)
  1. Vocabulary. I. Title.
  PE1449.F5537 2011
  428.1--dc22

                                        2011001467

Contents

Foreword

Mark Twain famously declared, "The difference between the almost right word and the right word is really a large matter—'tis the difference between the lightning bug and the lightning." The words that Robert Hartwell Fiske explains so carefully and caringly in *The Best Words* are the lightning words, the ones that illuminate the way for those who hear what you say and read what you write.

Less famously, Justice Oliver Wendell Holmes explained, "Language is the skin of living thought." Holmes recognized that just as your skin bounds and encloses your body, so does your word stock bound and enclose your mental life. *The Best Words* summons you to stretch your vocabulary by mastering uncommonly useful and usefully uncommon words. Accept that invitation and you will liberate your thoughts and your feelings, your speaking, your reading, and your writing—everything that makes up you.

—Richard Lederer,
author of *The Write Way* and
Anguished English

Introduction

As I have written elsewhere, "The point of learning new words is not to impress your friends or to seem more intelligent than they. The point is to see more, to understand more. An ever-increasing vocabulary uncovers connections, introduces spheres, and—in reminding us that there are words for all thoughts, all feelings, all behaviors, all things—upholds all humankind."*

The Best Words are words you actually will have occasion to use; they are not the sort of "weird" or "wonderful" words (such as "infrendiate" and "dromaeognathous") you might encounter only at insipid cocktail parties where one person tries to impress, or, as likely, insult, another. These words are meant to be spoken and written, and if you use them, you will learn them.

Since the average English speaker has a vocabulary of 10,000 to 20,000 words, and uses far fewer than that, learning these best words may be a very good use of your time—better, certainly, than reading about the mind-numbing tedium of your friends' daily lives on Facebook or Twitter.

The Best Words includes some of the best words the English language has to offer. Perhaps half the words in this book are regarded as "best" by *Vocabula Review* readers who nominated them, as well as others, for inclusion in *The Vocabula Review*'s "Best Words" webpage. (The comments that precede some of the best words were made by *Vocabula* readers who chose to make a case for their words being included in the "Best Words.") Others I myself regard as best, whether for their meaning, their pronunciation, or both their meaning and pronunciation.

I've also included 150 quiz questions at the end of the book so that, along with your using these words in your speaking and writing, you'll be able to test yourself on how well you remember their meanings.

—Robert Hartwell Fiske

---

* *Silence, Language, & Society*, Vocabula Books, 2008

The
BEST WORDS

abditory

(AB-di-tor-ee)

noun

a place to hide something, valuables, especially.

He spelled it. "Abditory. Place to hide things. Blaney says it's a scientific term. The office is full of them. I haven't had a chance before now since Tuesday night but with him up in Westchester I'm going to take a look. With a nut like Blaney you can never tell."
  —Rex Stout,
  Trouble in Triplicate, 1949

abstemious

(ab-STEE-mee-es)

adjective

1. eating and drinking in moderation. 2. sparingly used. 3. abstaining from wine.

An abstemious diet, during pregnancy, is most essential; as the habit of body, at that time, is usually feverish and inflammatory. I should, therefore, recommend abstinence from malt liquor, wine, and spirits; and, that but little meat be eaten. Rich soups and stews are very improper.
  —Pye Henry Chavasse,
  Advice to a Wife on the Management of Herself, 1854

The champagne was flowing for New Century Media's well-attended summer party, but Walsh was noticeably abstemious.
  —Tim Walker,
  "Bermuda's anxious wait to see if the Queen accepts their invitation," *Telegraph*, 2009

abstemiousness

(ab-STEE-mee-es-nes)

noun

"It refers to the bottom of the ocean . . . how great is that? The sinister 'abysso' recalls Tartarus, and overall conjures a gorgeous image of blind prognathous fish."

abyssopelagic

(ah-BIS-soh-pah-*laj*-ik)

adjective

of or relating to the deepest depths of the ocean floor.

Small organisms living in the first few centimeters of water below the surface form the neuston. The epipelagic zone, the uppermost waters of the open ocean, overlies the mesopelagic, or twilight zone. Beyond is the <u>abyssopelagic</u> zone of perpetual darkness, and deepest of all is the hadal region.
  —Marion Nixon and
  John Zachary Young,
  The Brains and Lives of Cephalopods, 2003

The abyssopelagic layer of an ocean is one of four layers that make up the aphotic zone, the portion of a body of water that little or no sunlight penetrates. The four layers, by increasing depth, are mesopelagic, bathypelagic, abyssopelagic, and hadopelagic (the deepest, darkest layer of the ocean).

adumbrate

(AD-um-*brate*)

verb

1. to give a sketchy outline of.
2. to prefigure indistinctly or disclose partially; foreshadow.
3. to darken or obscure partially.

A lithely tempestuous Scherzo leads to the declamatory, savage, even ponderous Intermezzo, elephants alternately plodding and ice-skating, though some of the melodic figures <u>adumbrate</u> the lugubrious march of the Finale.
  —Gary Lemco,
  "The Art of Dimitri
  Mitropoulos, Vol. 2,"
  Audiophile Audition, 2008

adumbration

(*ad*-um-BRAY-shen)

noun

1. the act of adumbrating.
2. a faint sketch; an imperfect representation.

agonal

(AG-ah-nel)

adjective

relating to agony, especially the agony of death.

The adjective *agonal* is used by clinicians to describe the visible events that take place when life is in the act of extricating itself from protoplasm too compromised to sustain it any longer. Like its etymological twin, *agony,* the word derives from the Greek *agon,* denoting a struggle.
　　—Sherwin B. Nuland,
　　How We Die, 1995

In their last few minutes, some people have an <u>agonal</u> heartbeat as well as respirations. It's just the agony of their body physically giving in, but sometimes that's misinterpreted. Someone, usually a hopeful family member, will say, "Oh, he's been breathing," while you look at the patient and she's taking one breath every fifteen seconds, hollow breaths not consistent with life.
　　—Eugene Richards,
　　The Knife and Gun Club, 1995

"It's crisp, lively, and fun to say. As with many of the best words, it sounds like its definition."

alacrity

(ah-LAK-rah-tee)

noun

1. cheerful willingness, readiness, or eagerness. 2. liveliness; enthusiasm.

Immediately he had finished tea he rose with <u>alacrity</u> to go out. It was this <u>alacrity</u>, this haste to be gone, which so sickened Mrs. Morel.
　　—D. H. Lawrence,
　　Sons and Lovers, 1913

The <u>alacrity</u> and enthusiasm shown by the premier Dominion were repeated in Australia and New Zealand.
　　—David Lloyd George,
　　War Memoirs of David Lloyd George, 1933

alacritous

(ah-LAK-rah-tes)

adjective

amanuensis

(ah-*man*-yoo-EN-sis)

noun

1. a secretary; a person who takes dictation. 2. a writer's assistant.

Her precaution was confirmed later when she learned that Mr. James liked his typists to be "without a mind"—and certainly not to suggest words to him, as some had done. It is doubtful whether he ever learned that Miss Bosanquet had trained herself especially to be his amanuensis.

—Leon Edel,
Henry James, 1972

This illumination captures in a nutshell how Hildegard saw her work as a mystic and theologian. She saw herself not as a religious author, but as an amanuensis of the divine. She reports that in her dramatic prophetic call of 1141 she heard: "O human, speak these things that you see and hear. And write them."

—William Harmless,
Mystics, 2007

ananias

(*an*-ah-NI-es)

noun

1. a Christian in the New Testament who was struck dead for lying. 2. a habitual liar.

The reds staged a planned demonstration of disruption and disorder at the mid-August hearings of the House Committee on Un-American Activities. Only a dupe or a liar—an Ananias, a Judas or a political Simple Simon—would try to persuade this editor, a "psy-war" analyst, that this was not a coordinated and treasonable operation.

—Anti-Communist Liaison,
Tactics, 1967

Ananias, a member of the Early Christian church in Jerusalem, dropped dead after lying to the Holy Spirit about withholding the profit from the sale of some land. A few hours later, his wife, Sapphira, told the same lie and promptly died.

anfractuous

(an-FRAK-choo-es)

adjective

full of twists and intricate turns; sinuous; tortuous.

Paint me a cavernous waste shore
Cast in the unstilted Cyclades,
Paint me the bold anfractuous rocks
Faced by the snarled and yelping
    seas.

Display me Aeolus above
Reviewing the insurgent gales
Which tangle Ariadne's hair
And swell with haste the perjured
    sails.
    —T. S. Eliot,
    "Sweeney Erect," 1920

The paintings were not as easy to reach as art books made them seem: the cave painter had to wriggle through a series of tight and <u>anfractuous</u> passageways, slippery and stifling, before dropping down into the utmost chamber, where he could attack, or create, the potent images.
    —John Updike,
    The Witches of Eastwick, 1984

anfractuosity

(an-*frak*-choo-OS-i-tee)

noun

animadversion

(*an*-ah-*mad*-VUR-zhen)

noun

1. harsh criticism. 2. a censorious remark.

In London, a man may live in splendid society at one time, and in frugal retirement at another, without <u>animadversion</u>.
    —James Boswell,
    The Life of Samuel Johnson,
    1791

Ought he to be subject to <u>animadversion</u> for soliciting the favor of Heaven on the same cause as that in which we fought the good fight, and acquired our independence?
    —Calvin Colton,
    *The Life of Henry Clay, the
    Great American,* 1846

animadvert

(an-ah-mad-VURT)

verb

to express criticism or censure; to speak out against.

antithalian

(an-tee-THAY-lee-an)

adjective

against enjoyment and laughter; opposed to fun or celebration.

Mr. Glowry, during his residence in London, had come to an agreement with his friend Mr Toobad, that a match between Scythrop and Mr. Toobad's daughter would be a very desirable occurrence. She was finishing her education in a German convent, but Mr. Toobad described her as being fully impressed with the truth of his Ahrimanic philosophy, and being altogether as gloomy and antithalian a young lady as Mr. Glowry himself could desire for the future mistress of Nightmare Abbey.

—Thomas Love Peacock,
Nightmare Abbey, 1818

apolaustic

(*ap*-ah-LOS-tik)

adjective

dedicated to enjoyment; pleasure loving; self-indulgent.

They lead an apolaustic life, residing in well-furnished houses, enjoying society, eating and drinking according to their pleasure, for they have only to form a wish and they immediately have any article of food they want; only it always makes its appearance in the form of a frog.

—*Fraser's Magazine for Town and Country,* 1850

It may be foolish of us to insist upon apolaustic happiness, but that is the kind of happiness that we can ourselves, most of us, best understand, and so we offer it to our ideal. In Royalty we find our Bacchus, our Venus.

—Max Beerbohm,
"King George the Fourth,"
The Works of Max Beerbohm,
1896

apollonian

(*ap*-ah-LOH-nee-an)

adjective

1. of or relating to the Greek god Apollo. 2. characterized by balance, clarity, and harmony. 3. noble; high-minded.

Borrowing the notion of a guardian angel, one might say that Holmes, with his <u>Apollonian</u> serenity and his irrepressible high spirits, was watched over by one of those grave-gay deities of the Greeks. What disappoints many about Holmes is the absence of passion and of a feeling of dedication, the lack of the pattern of torture and complexity such as generations following Dostoyevski and Nietzsche have come to expect of the modern hero.

    —Max Lerner, *Nine Scorpions in a Bottle*, 1994

Unlike more mercurial energetic types, <u>Apollonian</u> cool dancers behave as if they don't have to draw attention to themselves, feeling confident that attention will be paid to their magnetic manner.

    —Robert Greskovic,
    Ballet 101: A Complete Guide to Learning and Loving the Ballet, 1998

apollonic

(*ap*-ah-LON-ik)

adjective

The Apollonian and Dionysian are philosophical and literary concepts based on Greek mythology. Both sons of Zeus, Apollo is the god of the Sun, dreams, reason, serenity, and Dionysus is the god of music, ecstasy, wine, intoxication. The contrast between Apollo and Dionysus symbolizes principles of group behavior versus individualism, light versus darkness, peacefulness versus passion. Several writers have invoked this dichotomy in critical and creative works, including Friedrich Nietzsche, Carl Jung, Hermann Hesse, and others.

apotropaic

(ap-ah-troh-PEY-ik)

adjective

designed or intended to prevent evil or bad luck.

In Shakespearean comedy, enacted scenes often serve an <u>apotropaic</u> function: they work to ward off the danger that they represent, the representation itself ostensibly protecting the fictive characters (and by extension the actors and audience) from the dangers that usually give the plot its interest.
   —Susanne L. Wofford,
   Shakespeare Reread, 1994

apotropaism

(*ap*-ah-troh-PEY-iz-um)

noun

the use of magic or ritual to prevent evil or bad luck.

apotrope

(*ap*-ah-TROPE)

noun

amulets, talismans, and other symbols used to ward off evil or misfortune.

"It sounds so cool…, and how it's spelt looks awesome."

assuage

(ah-SWAJ)

verb

1. to make milder or less intense; to alleviate or ease. 2. to satisfy or relieve; appease. 3. to quiet, calm, or soothe.

When I could no longer serve them, the ministers have considered my situation. When I could no longer hurt them, the revolutionists have trampled on my infirmity. My gratitude, I trust, is equal to the manner in which the benefit was conferred. It came to me indeed, at a time of life, and in a state of mind and body, in which no circumstance of fortune could afford me any real pleasure. But this was no fault in the royal donor, or in his ministers, who were pleased, in acknowledging the merits of an invalid servant of the public, to <u>assuage</u> the sorrows of a desolate old man.
   —Edmund Burke,
   "A Letter," 1796

'Good gracious, no,' said Ashenden. 'All sensible people know that vanity is the most devastating, the most universal, and the most ineradicable of the passions that afflict the soul of man, and it is only vanity that makes him deny its power. It is more consuming than love. With advancing years, mercifully, you can snap your fingers at the terror and the servitude of love, but age cannot free you from the thralldom of vanity. Time can <u>assuage</u> the pangs of love, but only death can still the anguish of wounded vanity.'
—W. Somerset Maugham, "His Excellency," 1927

assuagement

(ah-SWAJ-ment)

noun

assuager

(ah-SWAJ-er)

noun

assuasive

(ah-SWA-siv)

adjective

atlantean

(*at*-lan-TEE-an)

adjective

1. of or relating to Atlas. 2. having great strength; having the strength of Atlas. 3. of or relating to Atlantis.

In the museum of San Giovanni in Laterano is a large mosaic pavement, taken from the Baths of Caracalla, on which are represented colossal heads and figures of some of the most celebrated gladiators of the day. Their brutal and bestial physiognomies, their huge, over-developed muscles, and <u>Atlantean</u> shoulders, their low, flat foreheads and noses, are hideous to behold, and give one a more fearful and living notion of the horror of those bloody games to which they were trained, than any description in words could convey. They make one believe that of all animals, none can be made so brutal as man.
—William W. Story, *Roba di Roma*, 1870

He was, it may be said, but the foremost wave in a mighty deluge, urged on by, as well as leading, those behind. Had he been as great morally as he was intellectually, he might probably have impressed a very different character upon the

French Revolution. He might have fostered and developed the spirit of liberty, without at the same time letting loose upon society the demons of licentiousness, of *persiflage,* and of blasphemy. But, with his vain and fickle character, it would have been as impossible for him to direct such a movement steadily, wisely, and beneficently, as it would have been to support the earth upon his shoulders. His was no <u>Atlantean</u> strength, capable of sustaining any great cause steadily and firmly: it was rather the fitful and uncertain strength of the wind, which, moved by forces not residing in itself, may at one moment refresh and revive the fainting traveler, and the next, heap the burning sands of the desert upon a perishing caravan,—may at one time carry prosperously across the main a vessel laden with precious treasure, and at another, overwhelm this same vessel in the depths of the ocean.
—Joseph Thomas,
Universal Pronouncing Dictionary of Biography and Mythology, 1908

"A word that means as it sounds, and a fluid pronunciation in keeping with its etymology: black bile."

atrabilious

(*at*-rah-BIL-yes)

adjective

1. melancholic; gloomy.
2. irritable; ill-natured; surly.

But the torch of taste has for the moment fallen into the hands of little men, anemic and <u>atrabilious</u>—men with neither laughter nor pity in their hearts.
—Richard Le Gallienne, as quoted in *The Publishers Weekly,* 1894

Yet at the same time he detected much of this same cheerfulness throughout the ship and something not very far from apparent unconcern, even in so <u>atrabilious</u> a soul as Killick.
—Patrick O'Brian, *The Wine-Dark Sea,* 1994

atrabiliary

(*at*-rah-BIL-ee-ah-ree)

adjective

atrabiliousness

(*at*-rah-BIL-yes-ness)

noun

Bb

babylonian

(*bab*-ah-LOH-nee-an)

adjective

1. pertaining to Babylon or Babylonia. 2. excessively luxurious, pleasure seeking, unrestrained, immoral, or wicked.

Sacred prostitution rapidly brought about a degeneration of <u>Babylonian</u> morals. The immense city, with its several million inhabitants, was given over to the most indescribable debauchery. Quintus Curtius, in his *History of Alexander the Great*, has outlined the libertinage of this great Assyrian metropolis. He remarks: "There can be nothing more corrupt than this people, none more learned in the arts of pleasures and voluptuousness. Fathers and mothers permitted their daughters to prostitute themselves to invited guests for money, while husbands were no less indulgent as regarded their wives."
—Lee Alexander Stone,
The Story of Phallicism, 1976

Disney prided itself on the distance it maintained from the rest of the movie industry and on the absence of <u>Babylonian</u> behavior around the lot.
—John Taylor,
Storming the Magic Kingdom,
1987

babylonian

(*bab*-ah-LOH-nee-an)

noun

An ancient empire of southern Mesopotamia, Babylonia (present-day Iraq) flourished under Hammurabi and Nebuchadnezzar II but was conquered by the Persians in 539 B.C. Its capital city, Babylon, has long been a symbol of excess and dissolution.

bacchant

(bah-KANT; BAK-ant)

noun

1. a follower of Bacchus, Greek god of wine. 2. a wine-loving, riotous reveler.

In those days, says Platter, it was customary for youths, who desired to learn, and especially to prepare themselves for the priesthood, to wander about, sometimes alone, but more frequently in groups. Being mostly very poor, they made shift to support themselves on the road and at school by begging. The bigger ones were called Bacchants, and the smaller, Sharpshooters. It was the duty of the bacchant to instruct the sharpshooter in the elementary branches; and the latter, in return, was bound to wait upon his senior, accompany him in his wanderings, beg for him, and when mendacity happened to be at a discount, sharpshoot, that is, in plain English, steal without scruple. The bacchant's share of the contract was only too frequently neglected; but woe was certain to befall the sharpshooter who failed in his. Consequently, while the drudges went about half-famished, begging and stealing, and thus graduating in all the smaller vices, the bacchants prepared for taking honours in the great ones by leading a jolly life, drinking, gaming, rioting, and robbing, too, whithersoever they went. An admirable method, truly, of training the spiritual pastors and masters of Christendom, and sufficiently explanatory of many curious mediaeval phenomena.

> —*The Cornhill Magazine,* "Out of School in the Middle Ages," 1869

bacchantes

(bah-KAN-teez)

noun, plural

bacchantic

(bah-KAN-tik)

adjective

bacchanalia

(*bak*-ah-NEY-lee-ah)

noun

1. the ancient Roman festival in honor of Bacchus, the god of wine. 2. a riotous, drunken revel; orgy.

bacchanalian

(*bak*-ah-NEY-lee-en)

adjective

banausic

(bah-NAW-sik)

adjective

1. mechanical; utilitarian; routine.
2. common; uncultured.

There is, however, something banausic in estimating the farmer's life by his profits. In a strictly utilitarian age, and among men who are perhaps at times slightly commonplace, and little moved by the lighter graces of art and poetry, it may be as well to point out to the farmer what a store of secondary pleasures (as he would deem them) his occupation discloses.
— Rev. M. G. Watkins,
"The Pleasures of Farming,"
The Gentleman's Magazine,
1891

By the fourth century, moreover, at least a vocal minority of the elite—Plato and Aristotle are prime examples—had come to condemn all manual labor, as well as commerce, on the grounds that it was "banausic": a word that, originally describing the handicrafts of artisans, came to mean "mechanical," and then "base," "common," or "in bad taste."
— Peter Green,
Alexander to Actium, 1993

Around the walls of the dissecting room were specimens in glass jars: livers, aortas, larynxes. At the far end was a wooden board on which were hung saws, chisels, knives and other banausic instruments of the trade.
— Sebastian Faulks,
Human Traces, 2005

Banausos (βάναυσος), an epithet for the class of laborers and artisans in Ancient Greece, became in the fifth-century BC, a term of disparagement, meaning "cramped in body" and "vulgar in taste." In the mid-nineteenth century, *banausos* was adapted into English as *banausic*.

baronial

(bah-ROH-nee-el)

adjective

1. of or relating to a baron.
2. befitting a baron. 3. stately,
imposing, or grand.

The brewery, his sturdy monument, still pays his *manes* tribute; it remains to this day strictly a family project, as he would have it. His descendants live on, true to his traditions, in the old grand, baronial manner.
—"The King of Beer,"
The American Mercury, 1929

This splendid baronial house of 1600 evolved over four centuries, being hugely enlarged by the successful Scottish architect William Bryce.
—David Pearce,
Conservation Today, 1989

"I just like the way it rolls off your tongue and isn't spelled 'bobble.' It's just ... cute."

bauble

(BAU-ble)

noun

1. a showy, usually cheap, ornament; trinket; gewgaw.
2. a jester's scepter.

SIR ANTHONY.—Hey! What the deuce have you got here?

ABSOLUTE. Nothing, sir—nothing.

SIR ANTHONY. What's this?—here's something damned hard.

ABSOLUTE. Oh, trinkets, sir! Trinkets!—a bauble for Lydia!

SIR ANTHONY. Nay let me see your taste.—[*Pulls his coat open, the sword falls.*] Trinkets!—a bauble for Lydia!—Zounds! sir-rah, you are not going to cut her throat, are you?
—Richard Brinsley Sheridan,
The Rivals, 1775

bellipotent

(bel-LIP-ah-tent)

adjective

mighty in war.

Many bulletins of these bloodless victories do still remain on record; and the whole province was once thrown in amaze, by the return of one of his campaigns; wherein it was stated, that though, like Captain Bobadil, he had only twenty men to back him, yet in the short space of six months he had conquered and utterly annihilated sixty oxen, ninety hogs, one hundred sheep, ten thousand cabbages, one thousand bushels of potatoes, one hundred and fifty kilderkins of small-beer, two thousand seven hundred and thirty-five pipes, seventy-eight pounds of sugar-plumbs, and forty bars of iron, besides sundry small meats, game, poultry, and garden stuff: An achievement unparalleled since the days of Pantagruel and his all-devouring army, and which showed that it was only necessary to let bellipotent Van Poffenburgh and his garrison loose in an enemy's country, and in a little while they would breed a famine, and starve all the inhabitants.

—Washington Irving,
A History of New York, 1809

The most prominent of the fabulous thieves in England is that bellipotent and immeasurable wag, Falstaff. If for a momentary freak, he thought it villainous to steal, at the next moment he thought it villainous not to steal.

—Leigh Hunt, *The Indicator*, 1845

In Herman Melville's novella *Billy Budd*, Billy Budd is a sailor aboard the British man of war, HMS *Bellipotent*.

benighted

(bi-NI-ted)

adjective

1. overtaken by darkness or night. 2. unenlightened; morally, intellectually, or socially ignorant.

And then they should do some good to the benighted, the most benighted, the fashionable benighted; they should perhaps make them furious—there was always some good in that.
　　—Henry James,
　　The Bostonians, 1886

To see these costs close up, visit the vast industrial wasteland that surrounds Detroit—the rusted, shuttered and socially benighted testament to the inability of America's car companies to keep pace with changing times.
　　—Gary Hamel,
　　"Should We Save Dying
　　Companies," *The Wall Street
　　Journal,* 2009

benightedness

(bi-NI-ted-ness)

noun

bestial

(BES-chel)

adjective

1. of or relating to beasts; beastly. 2. brutal or savage. 3. sexually depraved. 4. lacking intelligence, reason, or refinement.

And he was so unabashed and unrestrained. Wasn't it rather horrible, a man who could be so soulful and spiritual, now to be so—she balked at her own thoughts and memories: then she added—so bestial? So bestial, they two!—so degraded! She winced. But after all, why not? She exulted as well. Why not be bestial, and go the whole round of experience? She exulted in it. She was bestial. How good it was to be really shameful!
　　—D. H. Lawrence,
　　Women in Love, 1921

All werewolves are of evil disposition, having assumed a bestial form to gratify a bestial appetite, but some, transformed by sorcery, are as humane as is consistent with an acquired taste for human flesh.
　　—Ambrose Bierce,
　　The Devil's Dictionary, 1911

bibulous

(BIB-yah-les)

adjective

1. fond of alcoholic beverages.
2. absorbent.

The 31st Infantry had the distinction of being the only American infantry regiment in the Philippines out of 22,000 U.S. Army troops in the Philippines. But their reputation was more for <u>bibulosity</u> than for bravery; hence their moniker, the "Thirsty-First."
 —John Glusman,
 Conduct Under Fire, 2006

Ex-Soviet aircraft have long suffered mockery for their rickety construction, chewing-gum repair jobs, and <u>bibulous</u> crews.
 —Graeme Wood,
 "Prepared for the Worst,"
 The Atlantic Monthly, 2009

bibulousness

(BIB-yah-les-nes)

noun

bibulosity

(*bib*-yah-LOS-i-tee)

noun

boeotian (or beotian)

(bee-OH-shen)

adjective

1. of or relating to Boeotia or its people, who were reputed to be dull and stupid. 2. simple minded; dull; obtuse.

Ulrich von Hütten, a poet and a warrior, was a contemporary of Luther's. He is best known for an anonymous Latin pamphlet, styled "Letters of some Obscure Men," which had as much success at the time, as Pascal's celebrated "Provinciales," two centuries afterwards. It is a series of letters attributed to the pedantic supporters of the scholastic method, which then reigned paramount in the colleges and universities of Europe, exposing their ridiculous style, their <u>Beotian</u> ignorance, their hatred of innovation, their intolerance, presumption, and religious hypocrisy. The correspondence was considered for a time as genuine, and the scholastics themselves were deceived. But when the trick was discovered, anathemas fell on every side on Hütten's head, and his book was formally excommunicated by Rome. He wandered about to avoid persecution, and at last died in 1523, in a little island on the lake of Zurich, which is still known by his name—"Hütten's Grab," or Hütten's Grave.

—*The Foreign Quarterly Review*, 1838

boeotian

(bee-OH-shen)

noun

a simpleton.

Boeotia (also spelled Beotia), a region of ancient Greece, became politically significant after the Boeotian League was formed. Hostile to Athens, the League revolted against the city-state around 447 BC, and in the Peloponnesian War, Boeotia defeated Athens. Boeotia, very likely, came to be synonymous for the stupidity of its inhabitants after the Athenians promoted the idea that they were culturally superior to the Boeotians.

botryoidal

(*bot*-ree-OID-el)

adjective

shaped like or resembling a bunch of grapes.

For want of observing that the segmental surfaces of so-called reniform and botryoidal minerals are spheroidal, the really crystalline structure producing that external form has been overlooked, and in consequence, minerals have been continually described either as amorphous, or as mixtures of different substances, which are neither formless nor mingled, but are absolutely defined in structure, and absolutely homogeneous in substance.

—John Ruskin, "The Distinctions of Form in Silica," *The Works of John Ruskin,* 1906

botryoid

(BOT-ree-oid)

adjective

botryose

(BOT-ree-os)

adjective

bowdlerize

(BODE-ler-*ize*)

verb

to remove words or phrases from a book that are considered offensive or indecent; expurgate.

The Grimms sought to thoroughly sanitize and <u>bowdlerize</u> German and European folk tales so that they might be made appropriate for consumption by bourgeois children. The brothers Grimm understood that they were transforming entertaining tales into educational ones. They had a conscious agenda of perpetuating aristocratic norms and value systems.
　　—Marlene Wurfel,
　　"Walt Disney's TRUE
　　LOV$E," *Z Magazine*, 2006

But all Christians read like editors, holding in our hands a pencil that we do not fear to use whenever we see fit. Perhaps it is more true to say: all Christians are <u>bowdlerizers</u>. When we come to something we cannot or will not accept, we skip over it, hoping to find something we are happy to hold on to in the next chapter, the next verse, the next page, the next Evangelist.
　　—Mary Gordon,
　　Reading Jesus, 2009

bowdlerism

(BODE-ler-*iz*-em)

noun

bowdlerization

(BODE-ler-i-*zay*-shen)

noun

bowdlerizer

(BODE-ler-*iz*-er)

noun

The word *bowderlize* derives from Thomas Bowdler, an English physician, who, in 1818, published an expurgated edition of William Shakespeare's work, edited by his sister Harriet, intended for Victorian era women and children.

"More than any other word I can think of off the top of my head, bumbledom sounds exactly like what it means. I also enjoy the fact that it is derogatory, albeit playfully, towards bureaucrats exclusively."

bumbledom

(BUM-bel-dom)

noun

the world of petty, incompetent bureaucrats and other officials.

The outbreak of rabid <u>Bumbledom</u> which has burst upon the town during the last few months has again drawn public attention to the miserable condition of our licensing laws. The clumsy and brutal Act of Parliament, with the Holywell Street preamble, which came down to us from a time when reading and writing were not considered necessary accomplishments of a monarch, is again upon its trial.
　—John Hollingshead,
　Niagara Spray, 1890

A. S. Neill is a man of international reputation, and I hate the thought of what he may do to hold up British <u>Bumbledom</u> to ridicule throughout the civilized world.
　—Bertrand Russell,
　in a letter to Charles
　Trevelyan, *The Autobiography of Bertrand Russell,* 1967

bumptious

(BUMP-shes)

adjective

offensively assertive or pushy.

"Mrs. Avenel is the same as ever?"

"She holds her head higher, I think," said the landlord smiling. "She was always—not exactly proud like, but what I calls gumptious."

"I never heard that word before," said the Parson, laying down his knife and fork. "<u>Bumptious</u>, indeed, though I believe it is not in the dictionary, has crept into familiar parlance, especially amongst young folks at school and college."

"<u>Bumptious</u> is <u>bumptious</u>, and gumptious is gumptious," said the landlord, delighted to puzzle a parson. "Now the town beadle is <u>bumptious</u>, and Mrs. Avenel is gumptious."

"She is a very respectable woman," said Mr. Dale, somewhat rebukingly.

"In course, sir, all gumptious folks are; they value themselves on their respectability, and looks down on their neighbours."
　—Edward Bulwer-Lytton,
　My Novel, or Varieties in English Life, 1853

Yet speaking generally, and without any reference to this particular case, it is too true that when a man abandons himself to <u>bumptious</u> impulses, no matter in what respect, there is no annoyance and hardly any suffering that he will hesitate in causing to others if they stand in the way of his puffy pride. Cruelty is the natural issue of unchecked <u>bumptiousness</u>, and in a man's timid efforts to establish or increase his "importance," there is no sacrifice that he will not impose upon you — if he can.

—*Bentley's Miscellany*, 1866

bumptiousness

(BUMP-shes-nes)

noun

byzantine

(BIZ-an-*teen*)

adjective

1. scheming or devious. 2. highly complex; intricate.

Even the Nazis could not have devised a more devious and <u>Byzantine</u> method of dealing with their "undesirables."

—Institute for Social and
Cultural Communications,
Z Magazine

What distinguished it was its style: sentences that came in "clickety pop word bursts" or one of Cassady's trademark monologues. In fact, it was a forty-thousand-word letter from Cassady, relating the hilarious and <u>byzantine</u> complications of one of his Denver love affairs, that had crystallized *On the Road* for Jack.

—Jay Stevens,
Storming Heaven, 1998

Cc

cacology

(kah-KOL-ah-jee)

noun

1. bad choice or use of words.
2. socially unacceptable pronunciation.

The few words he says elsewhere in the play are all ridiculous; and the mistake of "paramour" for "paragon" is more appropriate to him than to Quince, who corrects the cacology of Bottom himself.
—William Maginn,
Miscellaneous Writings of the Late Dr. Maginn, 1856

As to *prose*, I don't know Addison's from Johnson's; but I will try to mend my cacology.

—Lord Byron,
in a letter to Thomas Moore,
The Life of Lord Byron, 1869

cairn

(KAIRN)

noun

a mound of stones set up as a marker, memorial, or burial site.

Rachel occupied herself in collecting one grey stone after another and building them into a little cairn; she did it very quietly and carefully.
—Virginia Woolf,
The Voyage Out, 1920

A long cairn of black stones marks the spot where a skeleton of *Ardipithecus ramidus* was found, its bones broken and scattered on a barren hillside. Erected as a monument to an ancient ancestor in the style of an Afar tribesman's grave, the cairn is a solitary marker in an almost sterile zone, devoid of life except for a few thorny acacia trees and piles of sifted sediment.
Ann Gibbons,
"*Ardipithecus ramidus:* Habitat for Humanity," *Science,* 2009

cairned

(KAIRNED)

adjective

caliginous

(kah-LIJ-i-nes)

adjective

dark and gloomy; obscure.

Here, selected from more, are a few 'fire-flies,'—not dancing or distracted, but authentic all, and stuck each on its spit; shedding a feeble glimmer over the physiognomy of those Fifteen <u>caliginous</u> Months, to an imagination that is diligent.
    —Thomas Carlyle,
    The Works of Thomas Carlyle,
    1898

'Was it very <u>caliginous</u> in the Metropolis?'

'Somewhat <u>caliginous</u>, but not altogether inspissated,' Lawrence replied gravely.
    —Robert Graves,
    Good-bye to All That, 1929

caliginosity

(kah-*lij*-i-NOS-i-tee)

noun

caliginousness

(kah-LIG-i-nos-nes)

noun

callosity

(kah-LOS-i-tee)

noun

1. the quality of being callous or unfeeling; hardheartedness. 2. a localized thickening of the skin.

All were described as "unfeeling." Relief advocates lamented that some people's bodies seemed immune to the involuntary responses that a neighbor's distress was supposed to trigger. They drew special attention to their adversaries' hearts, which were said to be as hard and inflexible as the metal coins they demanded as the nation's sole units of exchange. In May 1785, "Observator" claimed that the men at the helm of New Hampshire's government could not "feel for others, through a <u>callosity</u> of heart, which makes them insensible to any one's interest but their own."
    —Woody Holton,
    Unruly Americans and the Origins of the Constitution,
    2007

"I love the sound of the word, as well as the emotional connotations; it's haunting."

caterwaul

(KAT-er-wol)

verb

1. to wail or screech like a cat in heat. 2. to howl or make a harsh-sounding noise.

caterwaul

(KAT-er-wol)

noun

You dampen the ozone with your
  caterwaul
Your spotty skin makes marmalade
  decompose
Your insipid persiflage is off the wall
(And greenish stuff is standing 'neath
  your nose).
You harry and haggle like a
  scapegrace
And yet, I've grown accustomed to
  your face.
  —Clara Mitchell,
  New York Magazine Competi-
  tion, 1988

My point is that by moving here I had altered deliberately my relationship to the sexual caterwaul, and not because the exhortations or, for that matter, my erections had been effectively weakened by time, but because I couldn't meet the costs of its clamoring anymore, could no longer marshal the wit, the strength, the patience, the illusion, the irony, the ardor, the egoism, the resilience—or the toughness, or the shrewdness, or the falseness, the dissembling, the dual being, the erotic *professionalism*—to deal with its array of misleading and contradictory meanings.
  —Philip Roth,
  The Human Stain, 2001

caul

(KOL)

noun

a thin membrane, a portion of the amniotic sac, that sometimes covers a newborn mammal at birth.

I was born with a <u>caul</u>, which was advertised for sale, in the newspapers, at the low price of fifteen guineas. Whether sea-going people were short of money about that time, or were short of faith and preferred cork jackets, I don't know; all I know is, that there was but one solitary bidding, and that was from an attorney connected with the bill-broking business, who offered two pounds in cash, and the balance in sherry, but declined to be guaranteed from drowning on any higher bargain. Consequently the advertisement was withdrawn at a dead loss—for as to sherry, my poor dear mother's own sherry was in the market then—and ten years afterwards, the <u>caul</u> was put up in a raffle down in our part of the country, to fifty members at half-a-crown a head, the winner to spend five shillings. I was present myself, and I remember to have felt quite uncomfortable and confused, at a part of myself being disposed of in that way.
—Charles Dickens,
David Copperfield, 1850

The book remade me as a writer, because it appealed to something in me that had been waiting restlessly for a liberating touch. Inside me had been a romantic artist, a romantic poet, straining to emerge from some sort of <u>caul</u>.
—Clark Elder Morrow,
"Memory Between the Covers," *The Vocabula Review*, 2009

In medieval times, a caul enveloping a newborn's head was considered a sign of good luck. Eventually, it was thought that a baby's caul would give its owner luck and protect that person from drowning. Prized by sailors, cauls were often sold to them for large sums of money.

"I love the way this word sounds bitter and acidic just like its meaning."

caustic

(KOS-tik)

adjective

1. capable of burning or corroding by chemical action.
2. corrosive and bitingly sarcastic or witty; cutting.

Scrooge had often heard it said that Marley had no bowels, but he had never believed it until now.

No, nor did he believe it even now. Though he looked the phantom through and through, and saw it standing before him; though he felt the chilling influence of its death-cold eyes; and marked the very texture of the folded kerchief bound about its head and chin, which wrapper he had not observed before; he was still incredulous, and fought against his senses.

'How now!' said Scrooge, <u>caustic</u> and cold as ever.

'What do you want with me?'

'Much!'—Marley's voice, no doubt about it.

'Who are you?'

'Ask me who I was.'
   —Charles Dickens,
   A Christmas Carol, 1843

Houellebecq is the most famous novelist in France—last year's *La Carte et le Territoire* won the Prix Goncourt—yet he is perhaps less well known for his novels than his <u>causticity</u> on the subjects of sex and Islam. This <u>causticity</u> informs the novels but is not confined to them. In a 2001 interview Houellebecq called Islam "the stupidest religion" and was charged with incitement of religious hatred; he was later acquitted in court. As for women, his "reputation for getting drunk and making passes at his female interviewers" is widespread enough to have warranted nervous mention in the introduction to his recent *Paris Review* interview.
   —James Camp,
   "The Contemptibles and the Tapeworms: Houellebecq and BHL Correspond," *The Millions*, 2011

caustical

(KOS-ti-kel)

adjective

causticity

(kos-TIS-i-tee)

noun

chapfallen (or chopfallen)

(CHAP-fal-len)

adjective

dejected or dispirited; crestfallen.

HAMLET. Alas! poor Horatio. I knew him, my friend; a fellow of infinite jest, of most excellent fancy; he hath borne me on his back a thousand times; and now, where be your gibes now? your gambols? your songs? your flashes of merriment, that were wont to set the table on a roar? Not one now, to mock your own grinning? quite <u>chapfallen</u>? Now get you to my lady's chamber, and tell her, let her paint an inch thick, to this favour she must come; make her laugh at that.
—William Shakespeare,
The Tragedy of Hamlet, Prince of Denmark, circa 1589

Nothing in Nature is sneaking or <u>chap-fallen</u>, as somewhat maltreated or slighted, but each is satisfied with its being, and so is as lavender and balm. If skunkcabbage is offensive to the nostrils of men, still has it not drooped in consequence, but trustfully unfolded its leaf of two handsbreadth.
—Henry David Thoreau,
"Autumn," *The Journal of Henry David Thoreau*, 1854

chthonic

(THON-ik; kah-THON-ic)

adjective

relating to the underworld or the gods and spirits that dwell there; infernal.

The historical shift in the world's consciousness towards the masculine is compensated by the <u>chthonic</u> femininity of the unconscious.
—Carl Gustav Jung,
Collected Works: Psychology and Alchemy, 1953

The dragon is a <u>chthonian</u> being which has to be killed in order that mankind be born from the Earth; the Sphinx is a monster unwilling to permit men to live.
—Claude Lévi-Strauss,
Structural Anthropology, 1974

Bush still sings like a siren, an unleashed teen, a triumphant heroine, and she remains one of the few lyricists who can succeed with both surreal nonsense and elaborate conceits (Bush as rubber band, Bush as telescope, Bush as pigeon living on an angel's shoulder). Her best songs open up the rooms in her mind, but here only "Big Stripey Lie" dredges up her <u>chthonic</u> spunk ("It's a jungle in here"), and only the aching "Moments of Pleasure" rings with the obscure intimacy of her great ballads.

—Erik Davis,
Spin, 1993

chthonian

(THOH-nee-an; kah-THOH-nee-an)

adjective

Chthonic (from Greek χθών—chthōn, "earth; earthy; subterranean") pertains to spirits of the underworld. The pronunciation is troublesome for some English speakers. The *Oxford English Dictionary*, for instance, maintains that the first two letters should be pronounced kah-; other dictionaries, like the *American Heritage Dictionary*, consider these letters silent.

"I love the sibilance of its sound ... its elegant yet fun."

cicatrix

(SIK-ah-triks)

noun

new connective tissue that forms over a healing sore or wound; a scar.

There was no special difficulty about the second operation, but the integuments of the abdomen around the old cicatrix had become distended into a pouch by the gradual yielding of the cicatricial tissue, which was more marked in the peritoneal layer than in the integument.

—Alban Henry Griffiths Doran, *Clinical and Pathological Observations on Tumours of the Ovary, Fallopian Tube and Broad Ligament,* 1884

cicatrices

(*sik*-ah-TRI-seez)

noun, plural

cicatricial

(*sik*-ah-TRISH-el)

adjective

cicatricose

(si-KAT-tri-kos)

adjective

cinerea

(si-NIR-ee-ah)

noun

the gray matter of the brain and other nerve tissue.

In Banville's *The Sea*, winner of the Man Booker Prize in 2005, every page is dotted with words such as assegais, horrent, <u>cinereal</u>, knobkerrie, prelapsarian and mephitic.
   —Ted Gioia,
   "The New Canon,"
   Blogcritics.org, 2009

Therefore the greater the relative preponderance of alba (white matter) over <u>cinerea</u> (gray matter) the higher the intelligence; ... the more numerous the dendons, the greater the elaboration and individualization of the neuron.
   —American Anthropological Association, *American Anthropologist*, 1903

cinereal

(si-NIR-ee-el)

adjective

claque

(KLAK)

noun

1. a group of people hired to applaud a performer; professional applauders. 2. a group of obsequious admirers.

Near us some men, many of them officers, formed a sort of <u>claque</u> to cheer the advocates of Neutrality. They kept shouting, "Khanjunov! Khanjunov!" And whistled insultingly when the Bolsheviki tried to speak.
   —John Reed,
   Ten Days That Shook the World, 1919

"*Youuuu* asked *meeeee* a question, didn't you, and you got a *bigggg* laugh from your <u>claque</u>. And so now *youuuuu're* gonna keep *quiiiiet* and *lisssssten* to the answer. Okay"?
   —Tom Wolfe,
   The Bonfire of the Vanities, 1987

Claque (French for "clapping") originally referred to a body of professional applauders in French theaters. Jean Daurat, a sixteenth-century French poet, developed the claque by buying a number of tickets for a performance of one of his plays and giving them away in return for a promise of applause. In 1820, claques were systematized when a Paris agency opened to manage and supply *claqueurs*, as members of a claque are called. The manager of a theater or opera house was able to order any number of claqueurs. The practice spread to Italy, Vienna, London, and New York. Claques were also used as a form of extortion: singers were commonly contacted by the *chef de claque* before their debut and forced to pay a fee in order not to get booed.

clerisy

(KLER-i-see)

noun

the well-educated class; the literati; the intelligentsia.

Computers are far more than pragmatic tools. They initiate, they develop non-verbal methods and configurations of thought, of decision-making, even, one suspects, of aesthetic notice. Theirs is the new clerisy, a clerisy of the young and the very young who are, flexibly, pre- or counter-literate.
—George Steiner,
Real Presences, 1991

This class of people, what author Robertson Davies called the clerisy, comprised those who read books for pleasure. Not the professional critics or the scholars or the students who read because they have to, but rather, the people who read books as an end it itself. The true readers. The clerisy is the crucial element in any societal shift, and this is something every successful despot knows. The notion of the rabble-rousing mob of peasants overturning the social order is a myth; real revolutions begin with the clerisy.
—Will Ferguson,
Happiness, 2001

clochard

(kloh-SHAR)

noun

a beggar or tramp; vagrant.

A clochard is usually mistaken by non-Parisians for a beggar. He is however intensely respectable, but wants to have nothing to do with life as it is lived by his fellow citizens in stations below and above him. He despises the beggar, the criminal, the police, the bourgeoisie high and low, the aristocracy, the civil servant, the religious, the good and righteous, conservative and radical and all other political parties, with equal vehemence.
—Ludwig Bemelmans,
My Life in Art, 1958

One Paris clochard was a Foreign Legion officer, another a Tsarist colonel, a third, an intellectual who even as a clochard would give alfresco lectures on philosophy in the Latin Quarter for the price of a bottle of wine.
—John Ardagh,
The New French Revolution, 1968

cockalorum

(*kok*-ah-LOR-em)

noun

1. a self-important, boastful little man. 2. boastful talk; braggadocio. 3. high cockalorum; leapfrog.

SENATOR LT.-COL. GOULD. The honorable senator does not regard the members of the Commission as infallible?

SENATOR GIVENS. I do not. I think that the Chairman of the Commission is inclined to look upon himself as a sort of tin god—the Lord High Cockalorum of the Commonwealth, to whom everyone must bow down.
—Australian Parliament,
"Parliamentary Debates: Senate and House of Representatives," 1908

Then you have a beautiful calm without a cloud, smooth sea, placid, crew and cargo in smithereens, Davy Jones' locker, moon looking down so peaceful. Not my fault, old cockalorum.
—James Joyce,
Ulysses, 1937

collop

(KOL-op)

noun

1. a piece or slice of meat. 2. a fold of fat flesh on the body. 3. a small piece of something.

SHEPHERD. Fie, Joan, that
  thou wilt be so obstacle!
God knows thou art a <u>collop</u> of
  my flesh;
And for thy sake have I shed
  many a tear:
Deny me not, I prithee, gentle
  Joan.
   —William Shakespeare, *King
   Henry VI*, 1590

Worthy veal entrees include scaloppine valdostana (with mozzarella Dallas cheese) and Marsala, the latter a tender <u>collop</u> of veal slightly scented by Marsala wine. We finished this delightful meal with a fine raspberry tart, filled with lemony custard, in a thin, crumbly crust.
   —*Texas Monthly*, 1984

"I love it. It has a thick feel to the mouth."

conglomerate

(kon-GLOM-er-*it*)

noun

1. an organization consisting of different companies that deal with various business areas; a diversified corporation. 2. a mass of heterogeneous materials. 3. a rock consisting of pebbles and gravel held together by cement or clay.

These alternating masses are covered in the central parts, by a great thickness of red sandstone, <u>conglomerate,</u> and calcareous clay-slate, associated with, and passing into, prodigious beds of gypsum. In these upper beds, shells are tolerably frequent; and they belong to about the period of the lower chalk of Europe.
   —Charles Darwin,
   The Voyage of the Beagle, 1839

conglomerate

(kon-GLOM-er-*it*)

adjective

gathered into a mass; clustered.

concupiscent

(kon-KYOO-pi-sent)

adjective

1. having strong desires or appetites. 2. lustful; sensual.

When I went off, besides Book-debts never paid, but cross'd out and forgiven, I had as much Chalk scor'd up in my Bar upon your account, as would have whiten'd the Flesh of twenty Calves at *Rumford*, or have cur'd half the Town of the Heart-burn, that never were satisfied to this day; and as certainly as you are both damn'd, I would Arrest you here in the *Devil's* Name, but that I know a *Foreign-Plea*, or the Statute of *Limitation* are pleadable in defiance of me; and that Whore my Wife too, that us'd to open her Sluice and let in an inundation of Shabroons to gratify her Concupiscence, she lent her helping Buttock among you to shove on my Ruin, but if ever I catch the Strumpet in these Territories, I'll fear up the Bung-hole of her filthy Ferkin, but I'll reward her for her Bitching.
　—Thomas Brown,
　Letters from the Dead to the Living, 1707

I have no doubt, but that Immanuel had heard of that celebrated philosopher, who, so busied in looking in the skies, fell into a well. Enough—he did not deem it necessary, and future times must determine whether he was correct or not:—for a man to run all over the world, to see the Chinese eat opium—to peep into a harem, and discover what concupiscent fellows the Turks are—see whether the beastly Laplanders really do gorge whale-oil, and settle the matter as to the identity of the American Indian with other men.
　—*Desultoria: The Recovered Mss. of an Eccentric,* 1850

Call the roller of big cigars,
The muscular one, and bid him whip
In kitchen cups concupiscent curds.
Let the wenches dawdle in such dress
As they are used to wear, and let the
　boys
Bring flowers in last month's
　newspapers.
Let be be finale of seem.
The only emperor is the emperor of
　ice-cream.
　—Wallace Stevens,
　"The Emperor of Ice-Cream,"
　Harmonium, 1922

concupiscence

(kon-KYOO-pi-sens)

noun

coprolalia

(*kop*-rah-LAY-lee-ah)

noun

the uncontrolled or obsessive use of obscene or foul language.

Powerful sexual urges continued throughout this time, manifest as erotic dreams and nightmares, as frequent and somewhat compulsive masturbation, and (combined with aggression and perseveration) as a tendency to curse, to coprolalia, and to verbigerative sing-song pornoloquies with obscene refrains.

—Oliver W. Sacks,
Awakenings, 1999

Two terms related to *coprolalia* (from Greek κόπρος—*kopros,* "feces," and λαλιά—lalia, "to talk") are *copropraxia,* uncontrollably making obscene gestures, and *coprographia,* uncontrollably making obscene drawings or writings.

cotquean

(KOT-kween)

noun

1. a coarse or masculine woman.
2. a man who does work regarded as suitable only to women.

CAPULET. Come, stir, stir, stir!
   the second cock hath crow'd,
The curfew-bell hath rung, 'tis
   three o'clock.
Look to the baked meats, good
   Angelica:
Spare not for the cost.

LADY CAPULET. Go, you
   cot-quean, go,
Get you to bed; 'faith, You'll
   be sick to-morrow
For this night's watching.

CAPULET. No, not a whit. What!
I have watch'd ere now
All night for lesser cause, and
   ne'er been sick.

LADY CAPULET. Ay, you
   have been a mouse-hunt in
   your time;
But I will watch you from such
   watching now.

—William Shakespeare,
Romeo and Juliet, circa 1591

cuckquean (or cucquean)

(KUK-kween)

noun

a woman whose husband is
unfaithful.

While Beast instructs his fair and
   innocent wife
In the past pleasures of his sensual life,
Telling the motions of each petticoat,
And how his Ganymede moved and
   how his goat,
And now her, hourly, her own
   cuckquean makes
In varied shapes, which for his lust she
   takes:
What doth he else, but say, leave to be
   chaste,
Just wife, and, to change me, make
   woman's haste.
     —Ben Jonson,
     On Sir Voluptuous Beast,
     circa 1612

He watched her pour into the measure and thence into the jug rich white milk, not hers. Old shrunken paps. She poured again a measureful and a tilly. Old and secret she had entered from a morning world, maybe a messenger. She praised the goodness of the milk, pouring it out. Crouching by a patient cow at daybreak in the lush field, a witch on her toadstool, her wrinkled fingers quick at the squirting dugs. They lowed about her whom they knew, dewsilky cattle. Silk of the kine and poor old woman, names given her in old times. A wandering crone, lowly form of an immortal serving her conqueror and her gay betrayer, their common cuckquean, a messenger from the secret morning. To serve or to upbraid, whether he could not tell: but scorned to beg her favour.
     —James Joyce,
     Ulysses, 1937

deliquesce

(*del*-i-KWES)

verb

1. to melt away or dissolve; to disappear as if by melting.
2. to become liquid by absorbing moisture from the air.

Corde sat at his place again, read the first paragraph of "The Poet and the Violent Id" by Leon D. Gilchrist, Ph.D. He returned to the counter and borrowed a dictionary.

He tried again.

The poet, by which expansive term I am taking the liberty of referring to anyone who creates fictional modes with words, is himself a creation of the society in which he lives. Indeed, it is the obligation of the poet to <u>deliquesce</u> ...

"<u>Deliquese</u>."

Corde marked his place in the journal with his elbow and thumbed through the dictionary. The "levitate"/"licentious" page fell out. He stuffed it back between "repudiate"/"resident" and "residual"/"response."

"<u>Deliquese</u>, v. To melt by absorbing moisture or humidity contained in the air."

Okay. Good.

... obligation of the poet to <u>deliquesce</u> *so that he might permeate all aspects of society....*
    —Jeffery Deaver,
    The Lesson of Her Death, 1994

deliquescence

(*del*-i-KWES-ence)

noun

deliquescent

(del-i-KWES-ent)

adjective

demimonde

(DEM-ee-*mond*)

noun

1. a class of women supported by wealthy lovers. 2. the world of prostitution. 3. any group on the fringes of society regarded as not wholly respectable.

Horace and the elegiac poets present a society much given to parties and love affairs with women and boys of charm and elegance, belonging to what the nineteenth century would have called the demimonde; and if the expression 'demimonde' is unfamiliar to modern readers, it is because modern Western society has lost in the course of this century a recognizable sub-culture of easy virtue with its own rules and conventions, catering outside marriage to the pleasures of 'respectable' society.

    —Colin Michael Wells,
    The Roman Empire, 1984

Yet Hefner's monthly still has pretensions of cultural relevance, even if that culture is locked in the James Bond–accented lounge-lizard demimonde of the 1960s.

    —Bruce Watson,
    "Marge Simpson poses nude,
    but Playboy keeps on singing
    the blues," *Daily Finance*, 2009

demimondaine

(*dem*-ee-mon-DANE)

noun

a woman of the demimonde; a prostitute; demirep.

The demimonde referred to a class of women who were supported by wealthy lovers. Though commonplace in the mid- and late-nineteenth century in France and England, the demimonde began to disappear in the twentieth century as women became more independent. The term then referred to "starving artists" and others who were ostracized because of their failure, or unwillingness, to achieve material success.

"Pretty and evocative; the texture of light above running water."

diaphanous

(di-AF-ah-nes)

adjective

1. delicate or translucent. 2. fragile or insubstantial.

That the last circumference of the universe is but the bubble of the chaos and pellicle arising from the grosser foundation of the first matter, containing all the higher and <u>diaphanous</u> bodies under it, is no affirmation of mine; but that bubbles on watery or fluid bodies are but the thin gumbs of air, or a <u>diaphanous</u> texture of water arising about the air, and holding it awhile from eruption.
—Sir Thomas Browne,
The Works of Sir Thomas Browne, 1852

diaphaneity

(*di*-af-ah-NEY-i-tee)

noun

diaphanousness

(di-AF-ah-nes-nes)

noun

dicephalous

(di-SEF-ah-les)

adjective

having two heads; two-headed.

There are acephalous, <u>dicephalous</u>, and disomatous monsters; others again, like the Siamese twins, have two bodies united by a mere band of integument.
—Alfred Swaine Taylor and Edward Hartshorne,
Medical Jurisprudence, 1856

Rather than dismiss people like Nicolas Ferry, the King of Poland's court dwarf, and the <u>dicephalous</u> Tocci brothers, as freaks, I have regarded them as human beings, born with sometimes appalling congenital deformities, and tried to chronicle their lives and vicissitudes as closely as possible.
—Jan Bondeson,
The Two-Headed Boy and Other Medical Marvels, 2004

dicephalism

(di-SEF-ah-liz-em)

noun

dicephalic

(di-sah-FAL-ik)

adjective

dicephalus

(di-SEF-ah-les)

noun

1. conjoined twins with two heads. 2. a monster with two heads.

> *Polycephaly* means "having more than one head." The term comprises bicephaly and dicephaly, which both refer to two-headedness.

dyspeptic

(dis-PEP-tik)

adjective

1. relating to or having indigestion. 2. having a morose disposition; grouchy; bad-tempered.

Nay, we should expect that the gall, and the hemlock, and the wormwood, and the vinegar, would be mixed together on his pages. Such a mixture would not, indeed, be very palatable to a healthy appetite. But nervous ailments produce a morbid appetite in the mind, as well as in the body; and hence, such disgusting mixtures are greedily devoured. In short, the dyspeptic writer is apt to find a dyspeptic community to relish his productions.
—Edward Hitchcock,
Dyspepsy Forestalled and Resisted, 1831

Though she's called Madam, Black's Jacques also wears male clothes and saunters through the Forest of Arden more as a slightly dyspeptic philosopher than as a grumpy misanthrope.
—Evan Henerson,
"To Arden with Aquila—
Review of As You Like It,"
Examiner.com, 2009

ebullient

(i-BOOL-yent)

adjective

1. enthusiastic; lively or high-spirited. 2. boiling or bubbling.

Talk of this kind for years before the war had not increased friendliness for Germany. "We often got on the world's nerves," admitted Bethmann-Hollweg, by frequently proclaiming Germany's right to lead the world. This, he explained, was interpreted as lust for world dominion but was really a "boyish and unbalanced ebullience." The world somehow failed to see it that way. There was a stridency in the German tone that conveyed more menace than ebullience.
 —Barbara W. Tuchman,
  The Guns of August, 1962

Talk of this kind for years before the war had not increased friendliness for Germany. "We often got on the world's nerves," admitted

Bethmann-Hollweg, by frequently proclaiming Germany's right to lead the world. This, he explained, was interpreted as lust for world dominion but was really a "boyish and unbalanced ebullience." The world somehow failed to see it that way. There was a stridency in the German tone that conveyed more menace than ebullience.
 —Barbara W. Tuchman,
  The Guns of August, 1962

Vivid yellows are seen as active, ebullient, sparkling with enthusiasm and youthful vigor.
 —Leatrice Eiseman,
  Colors for Your Every Mood, 2000

Delegates emerging from a conference tend in my experience to be in one of two moods: resentful, or ebullient. These were ebullient, but bellicose. They had extravagant hopes, but also enemies.
 —John Le Carré,
  The Mission Song, 2006

ebullience

(i-BOOL-yence)

noun

ebulliency

(i-BOOL-yen-see)

noun

edentulous

(ee-DEN-choo-les)

adjective

having no teeth; toothless.

I read that the state government of Perak in Malaysia has decided to supply 46 priests with false teeth. This is not because the <u>edentulous</u> clerics can't cope with tough kebabs, or whatever nutrients Muslim divines rely upon to keep the vile body attached to the immortal soul. Not a bit of it—the dentures are being supplied because of complaints received from the citizenry. The toothless ecclesiastics are to have their mouths refurbished because, lacking gnashers, they are unable to chant verses from the Koran clearly, to the evident detriment of the fabric of Malaysian society.
　　—Donald Gould,
　　New Scientist, 1985

<u>Edentulous</u> Support Society, the country's first support group for people without teeth was launched recently. The group aims to offer <u>edentulous</u> people (people without teeth) support and guidance, and also help them identify dental solutions.
　　—Deepa Suryanarayan,
　　"Now, you will say cheese with ease," *Daily News & Analysis,* 2009

edentulism

(ee-DEN-choo-liz-em)

noun

toothlessness

The teeth play a principal role in speech. Some letter sounds require the lips, tongue, or both lips and tongue to make contact with teeth for correct pronunciation of the sound. The fricative consonant sounds of the English language *s*, *z*, *x*, *d*, *n*, *l*, *j*, *t*, *th*, *ch*, and *sh* are achieved with tongue-to-tooth contact, and the fricative *f* and *v* are achieved through lip-to-tooth contact. Properly enunciating these sounds is very difficult for edentulous people.

ennead

(EN-ee-*ad*)

noun

1. a group of nine. 2. the number nine.

Another combination of gods is the ennead, or circle of nine gods. The ennead first appears in the fourth Dynasty (about 3000 BC).
—F. C. H. Wendel,
History of Egypt, 2008

enneadic

(*en*-ee-AD-ik)

adjective

The Ennead was a group of nine deities in Egyptian mythology. The Ennead consisted of the sun god Atum, his children Shu and Tefnut, their children Geb and Nut, and their children Osiris, Isis, Set, and Nephthys.

epicene

(EP-i-seen)

adjective

1. having both male and female characteristics. 2. effeminate. 3. sexless; neuter. 4. having only one grammatical form to indicate either sex.

Along the garden-wall the bees
With hairy bellies pass between
The staminate and pistilate,
Blest office of the epicene.

Sweeney shifts from ham to ham
Stirring the water in his bath.
The masters of the subtle schools
Are controversial, polymath.
—T. S. Eliot,
"Mr. Eliot's Sunday Morning Service," 1920

"Mr. Jones says that to make love to Miss Saunders would be epicene."

"Epicene? What's that?"

"Shall I tell him, Mr. Jones? or will you?"

"Certainly. You intend to, anyway, don't you?"

"Epicene is something you want but can't get, Joe."
—William Faulkner,
Soldiers' Pay, 1925

The term épicène comes from the language of the grammarians: épicène is a word that may refer to either sex. In French, *enfant* "child," *girafe* "giraffe," *souris* "mouse" are épicènes. Now it is also used to designate things that would be equally suitable for both sexes: an "epicene education" would be an education that would serve the material and moral interest of girls and boys equally. There are "unisex" hairdressers; the term épicène is the equivalent of this word, but in literary language.

—Michèle Le Doeuff,
The Sex of Knowing, 2003

epicene

(EP-i-*seen*)

noun

an epicene person or thing.

epicenism

(EP-i-*seen*-iz-em)

noun

erinaceous

(*er*-i-NEY-shes)

adjective

relating to or resembling a hedgehog.

We came together, not to combat, but to share, one another's interests; not to promulgate our own views, but to tempt others to the expression of theirs; not as erinaceous propagandists, but as gentle lovers of our kind.

—Price Collier,
"Extemporaneous Sociability,"
in *The North American Review,*
1907

At that time, when I had just started working in the office of *Vanity Fair*, to which he was a distinguished contributor, I saw his more erinaceous side. I provoked him to ferocity one day by asking him who the Father Duffy was to whom he was in the habit of referring as if he were the Apostle Paul.

—Edmund Wilson,
"Alexander Woollcott of the Phalanx," in *Classics and Commercials,* 1950

erumpent

(i-RUM-pent)

adjective

bursting forth or through a surface.

Rhizopogons are not only the most ubiquitous of all the hypogeous (underground) fungi, they are also among the most visible. Many are erumpent (i.e., they burst through the surface of the ground at maturity); others are excavated by squirrels.

—David Arora,
Mushrooms Demystified, 1986

She has erumpent breasts, and her perfume smells like a three-day weekend. I introduce myself as a writer on assignment, and she offers to give me a tour and I drool in acceptance. She is barefoot and walks on her tiptoes.

—Jayson Gallaway,
Diary of a Viagra Fiend, 2004

etiolate

(EE-tee-ah-late)

verb

1. to cause a plant to whiten or wither by preventing exposure to light. 2. to cause to appear pale and sickly; to drain of color or strength. 3. to weaken by arresting the growth or development of.

When a gardener wishes to etiolate, that is, to blanch, soften, and render juicy a vegetable, as lettuce, celery, etc. he binds the leaves together, so that the light may have as little access as possible to their surfaces. In like manner, if we wish to etiolate men and women, we have only to congregate them in cities, where they are pretty securely kept out of the sun, and where they become as white, tender, and watery as the finest celery.

—James Johnson,
Change of Air; Or, The Diary of a Philosopher in Pursuit of Health and Recreation Illustrating the Beneficial Influence of Bodily Exercise, Change of Scene, Pure Air and Temporary Relaxation as Antidotes to the Wear and Tear of Education and Avocation, 1831

Yet she would never come to him—she daren't, she daren't, so much was against her. And the little etiolated body of her husband, city-branded, would possess her, and his little, frantic penis would beget another child in her.

—D. H. Lawrence,
"Sun," *The Woman Who Road Away and Other Stories*, 1928

etiolated

(EE-tee-ah-*lay*-ted)

adjective

etiolation

(*ee*-tee-ah-LAY-shen)

noun

eviscerate

(i-VIS-ah-*rate*)

verb

1. to remove the entrails from; disembowel; gut. 2. to remove an essential part of something. 3. to remove an organ or the contents of an organ.

There are those who wash out the abdomen, and those who wipe it out; those who eviscerate the patient, and those who handle the entrails as little as possible; those who drain the abdomen, and those who sew it up; those who insist upon a particular position of the patient to aid drainage, and those who disregard this factor; those who feed by the mouth, and those who feed by the rectum; those who drain the distended gut by enterostomy; and those who inject into it cathartics and food. Some of these practices I endorse; others I condemn.

—James G. Mumford, M.D.,
"Certain Diseases of the Peritoneum," *New York Medical Journal*, 1907

There are flood and drouth
Over the eyes and in the mouth,
Dead water and dead sand
Contending for the upper hand.
The parched <u>eviscerate</u> soil
Gapes at the vanity of toil,
Laughs without mirth.
      This is the death of earth.
  —T. S. Eliot,
  "Little Gidding," 1945

evisceration

(i-*vis*-ah-RAY-shen)

noun

eviscerator

(i-*vis*-ah-RAY-tor)

noun

factotum

(fak-TOH-tum)

noun

an assistant or employee who has a wide range of duties.

I had almost forgotten Monee, the grinning old man who prepared our meal. His head was a shining, bald globe. He had a round little paunch, and legs like a cat. He was Po-Po's <u>factotum</u>—cook, butler, and climber of the bread-fruit and cocoa-nut trees; and, added to all else, a mighty favourite with his mistress; with whom he would sit smoking and gossiping by the hour.
 —Herman Melville,
 Omoo, 1847

"As if all this weren't enough, he's got a <u>factotum</u> who's another eccentric."

"What do you mean, a <u>factotum</u>?"

"I don't know how to explain it to you. He employs a sort of all-purpose go-between who waits on him hand and foot as well as keeping an eye on the business. He's everything rolled into one: a friend, an errand boy, a chauffeur."
 —Isaac Bashevis Singer,
 Shadows on the Hudson, 1997

Factotum derives from the Latin imperative *fac totum* ("do or make everything").

"It's just so upper crust."

fastidious

(fah-STID-ee-es)

1. having or requiring meticulous attention to detail; excessively particular. 2. difficult to please.

"I suspect," said Elinor, "that to avoid one kind of affectation, Edward here falls into another. Because he believes many people pretend to more admiration of the beauties of nature than they really feel, and is disgusted with such pretensions, he affects greater indifference and less discrimination in viewing them himself than he possesses. He is <u>fastidious</u> and will have an affectation of his own."

    —Jane Austen,
    Sense and Sensibility, 1811

fastidiousness

(fah-STID-ee-es-nes)

noun

fat-witted

(FAT-*wit*-id)

adjective

thick-headed; dull-witted; stupid.

FALSTAFF. Now, Hal, what time of day is it, lad?

PRINCE HENRY. Thou art so <u>fat-witted</u>, with drinking of old sack and unbuttoning thee after supper and sleeping upon benches after noon, that thou hast forgotten to demand that truly which thou wouldst truly know. What a devil hast thou to do with the time of the day? Unless hours were cups of sack and minutes capons and clocks the tongues of bawds and dials the signs of leaping-houses and the blessed sun himself a fair hot wench in flame-coloured taffeta, I see no reason why thou shouldst be so superfluous to demand the time of the day.

    —William Shakespeare,
    King Henry VI, 1590

feckless

(FEK-lis)

adjective

1. lacking purpose; ineffective; weak or feeble. 2. worthless; irresponsible.

The beasts stood with heads lowered dejectedly against the wooden hoot-pieces of their stalls. Graceless, Pointless, <u>Feckless</u>, and Aimless awaited their turn to be milked. Sometimes Aimless ran her dry tongue, with a rasping sound sharp as a file through silk, awkwardly across the bony flank of <u>Feckless</u>, which was still moist with the rain that had fallen upon it through the roof during the night, or Pointless turned her large dull eyes sideways as she swung her head upwards to tear down a mouthful of cobwebs from the wooden runnet above her head.

—Stella Gibbons,
Cold Comfort Farm, 1932

Come, what else is there? What other end if you don't make the end? Make your own bright end in the darkness of this dying world, this foul and <u>feckless</u> place, where you know as well as I that nothing ever really works, that you were never once yourself and never will be or he himself or she herself and certainly never once we ourselves together. Come, close it out before it closes you out because believe me life does no better job with dying than with living. Close it out. At least you can do that, not only not lose but win, with one last splendid gesture defeat the whole foul <u>feckless</u> world.

—Walker Percy,
The Second Coming, 1999

fecklessness

(FEK-lis-nes)

noun

florilegium

(*flor*-ah-LEE-jee-um)

noun

1. a collection of literary extracts; an anthology. 2. a collection of flowers or pictures of them.

We have made but a small <u>florilegium</u> from Mr. Hazlitt's remarkable volumes.

> —James Russell Lowell,
> *The Writings of James Russell Lowell*, 1892

Florilegium (plural *florilegia*) is formed from the Latin *flos*, "flower," and *legere*, "to gather": literally, a gathering of flowers or collection of extracts from a larger work.

"Its synonym, 'dandified,' is just as cool."

foppish

(FOP-ish)

adjective

of or relating to a fop; dandified; excessively fastidious in clothing and manners.

FOOL. Why—after I have cut the egg i' th' middle and eat up the meat—the two crowns of the egg. When thou clovest thy crown i' th' middle, and gavest away both parts, thou borest thy ass o' th' back o'er the dirt. Thou hadst little wit in thy bald crown when thou gavest thy golden one away. If I speak like myself in this, let him be whipped that first finds it so.

> (*sings*) Fools had ne'er less wit in a year,
> For wise men are grown <u>foppish</u>.
> They know not how their wits to wear,
> Their manners are so apish.
> —William Shakespeare,
> *King Lear*, circa 1608

The Arts & Entertainment Network is the prime operative in staking out airwave Lebensraum, reliably offering hours and hours of war documentaries each week, many of them Hitler-related. ...

Fortunately, during those rare time slots when A&E is instead airing *A&E's An Evening at the Improv* or sundry British foppery, other networks pick up the slack, creating, in effect, a dream come true for white supremacists and adolescent war-game buffs: the Hitler Channel!

—David Kemp,
"The Hitler Channel: All Adolf, All the Time," *Spy*, 1990

foppishness

(FOP-ish-nes)

noun

fop

(FOP)

noun

a man excessively concerned about his clothing and manners; a dandy.

foppery

(FOP-er-ee)
noun

1. foolish behavior; folly. 2. the clothing, manners, or behavior of a fop.

frippery

(FRIP-i-ree)

noun

1. showy finery or ornamentation. 2. pretentious ostentation. 3. something trivial or tawdry. 4. old cast-off clothes.

Like certain writers of our own, Mr. Chapman is so anxious to put off the frippery of conventional literary diction that he assumes with undue readiness the frippery of slang. For instance, it comes upon us with a jar, outside the columns of a newspaper, to be told, as Mr. Chapman does not hesitate to tell us, that this or that would "write up" into a monograph. Would "write up"; does not this smack somewhat of the "barbaric yawp"?

—"Transatlantic Criticism,"
The Academy, 1898

But however small, in the scheme of things, the frippery of moats and duck-houses has had a genuine impact on public reaction, on the speed and depth of our disgust.

—Harry de Quetteville,
"Second World War Anniversary," *Telegraph*, 2009

fuliginous

(fyoo-LIJ-i-nes)

adjective

1. sooty; colored by or as if by soot or smoke. 2. dark; dusky. 3. obscure or murky.

When vegetable bodies are made to burn, there is always more or less of a <u>fuliginous</u> substance formed; but this <u>fuliginous</u> substance is no other than a bituminous body in that subtilised state in which it is indefinitely divided, and may be mixed uniformly with any mass of matter equally subtilised with itself.
　—James Hutton,
　Theory of the Earth, Volume 1,
　1785

In the old Marquis there dwells withal a crabbedness, stiff cross-grained humor, a latent fury and <u>fuliginosity</u>, very perverting; which stiff crabbedness, with its pride, obstinacy, affectation, what else is it at bottom but want of strength? The real quantity of our insight,—how justly and thoroughly we shall comprehend the nature of a thing, especially of a human thing,—depends on our patience, our fairness, lovingness, what strength soever we have: intellect comes from the whole man,

as it is the light that enlightens the whole man.
　—Thomas Carlyle,
　"Mirabeau," 1837

He had a large, handsome head, and a large, sallow, seamed face—a striking, significant physiognomic total, the upper range of which, the great political brow, the thick, loose hair, the dark, <u>fuliginous</u> eyes, recalled even to a generation whose standard had dreadfully deviated the impressive image, familiar by engravings and busts, of some great national worthy of the earlier part of the mid-century.
　—Henry James,
　The Ambassadors, 1909

fuliginosity

(fyoo-LIJ-i-*nos*-i-tee)

noun

"Mordecai Richler used this word, and I like it a lot—the meaning especially."

fulminate

(FUL-mi-*nate*)

verb

1. to utter a scathing verbal attack or denunciation. 2. to explode or detonate violently.

Carlyle fought a Giant Despair all his life, and never for a moment gave an inch of ground. Indeed, so far as the upshot of his life was concerned, the amount of work actually done, and its value as a tonic and a spur to noble endeavor of all kinds, it is as if he had fought no Giant Despair at all, but had been animated and sustained by the most bright and buoyant hopes. The reason of this probably is that his gloom and despair did not end in mere negation. If he <u>fulminated</u> an Everlasting No, he also <u>fulminated</u> an Everlasting Yes.

    —John Burroughs,
    Indoor Studies, 1889

The Baron's change of religious views caused the greatest excitement throughout the country. The liberal newspapers published <u>fulminatory</u> articles; flaming protests were made in the clubs against the surreptitious propaganda of Rome.

    —Jacob Wassermann,
    The Goose Man, 1922

Lying in the dark, <u>fulminating</u>, I recited aloud the number I was to call if I had a heart attack.

    —Mordecai Richler,
    Barney's Version, 1997

fulmination

(*ful*-mi-NEY-shen)

noun

fulminator

(FUL-mi-*ney*-tor)

noun

fulminatory

(FUL-mi-nah-*tor*-ee)

adjective

fustigate

(FUS-ti-*gate*)

verb

1. to beat or cudgel; to punish harshly. 2. to criticize severely.

A dead Catholic Church is not allowed to lie dead; no, it is galvanised into the detestablest death-life; whereat Humanity, we say, shuts its eyes. For the Patriot women take their hazel wands, and <u>fustigate</u>, amid laughter of bystanders, with alacrity: broad bottom of Priests; alas, Nuns too reversed, and *cotillons retrousses*! The National Guard does what it can: Municipality 'invokes the Principles of Toleration;' grants Dissident worshippers the Church of the Theatins; promising protection. But it is to no purpose: at the door of that Theatins Church, appears a Placard, and suspended atop, like Plebeian Consular fasces,—a Bundle of Rods!
    —Thomas Carlyle,
    The French Revolution:
    A History, 1837

fustigatory

(FUS-ti-gah-tor-ee)

adjective

fustigation

(*fus*-ti-GEY-shen)

noun

fustigator

(fus-ti-GEY-tor)

noun

Gg

gehenna

(gi-HEN-ah)

noun

1. a place or state of misery and torment. 2. hell.

The word *hell* in English is the word *gehenna* in Greek. Gehenna is a reference to the Valley of Hinnom, a ravine on the south side of the city of Jerusalem. This valley was the site over the years of many violent and horrible deaths, and it came to be viewed as cursed. By Jesus' day it had become the town dump. Garbage, trash, wild animals fighting over scraps of food, a fire burning—a place of waste and destruction.

—Rob Bell,
Velvet Elvis, 2006

"I love the way it rolls off your tongue when pronounced—try it!"

globule

(GLOB-yool)

noun

a small spherical body; a small drop of liquid.

Take a basin full of water; put into it a globule of metal, or a stone, which will settle at the bottom. Place a bowl over this globule, either made of metal so as to sink of itself, or forced down with the hand. If the globule be so small that the air will willingly admit of condensation enough to take the globule within the bowl, it will condense itself quietly, and there will be no other motion; but if the globule be larger than the air can well bear, the air will resist, raise up one side of the bowl, and escape in bubbles.

—Francis Bacon,
Topics of Inquiry Respecting Light and Luminous Matter,
circa 1600

globular

(GLOB-yah-ler)

adjective

gormandize

(GOR-man-*dize*)

verb

to eat gluttonously or ravenously; to devour.

Charley swallows a great gulp of tea in token of submission and so disperses the Druidical ruins that Miss Smallweed charges her not to gormandize, which "in you girls," she observes, is disgusting.
—Charles Dickens,
Bleak House, 1853

I know, my dear Kit, that you never were a gormandizer, nor a sot; neither surely was I—but it matters not,—the most abstemious of us all have gone through fearful trials, and I have not skill in figures to cast up the poisonous contents of my hapless stomach for nearly three-score years.
—"Letter from an Elderly Gentleman to Mr Christopher North," *Blackwood's Edinburgh Magazine,* 1820

gormandizer

(GOR-man-*diz*-er)

noun

1. a greedy, ravenous eater; a glutton; a gourmand. 2. a greedy person.

"The word itself is dignified and poised; besides, isn't it funny to have a big, impressive word about big, impressive words?"

grandiloquent

(gran-DIL-ah-kwent)

adjective

1. using high-flown, pompous, bombastic words. 2. overblown or pretentious.

"I want to shoot your pistol again," she said. "Will you let me?"

"I am at your service today," he replied, affecting a grandiloquent sweep of his hat. "Whatever you want to do."
—Bram Stoker,
Dracula, 1897

A walk along the law lords corridor in the Palace of Westminster this summer was a sorry affair, with the bustle gone, the offices gutted and the empty rooms eyed up by envious peers. But to step across Parliament Square and enter the new Supreme Court, set amid the sand-blasted stone of the former Middlesex Guildhall, was to sense the anticipation of power. Here all was new and sleek with thick coatings of legal, black leather. Grandiloquent quotations and

wispy crests lined the glass walls,
bizarrely offset by a gaudy carpet
design by Sir Peter Blake.
    —Tristram Hunt,
    "The Supreme Court Is a
    Perfectly English Idea," *The
    Times*, 2009

grandiloquence

(gran-DIL-ah-kwence)

noun

hebdomad

(HEB-dah-*mad*)

noun

1. the number seven. 2. a group of seven people or things. 3. a period of seven days; a week.

Belief in hebdomadism (the sacredness of the number seven) was widespread. The Jewish account of creation in Genesis specifies seven days. The seven-day week is physiologically adequate; six days of labor and one of rest is a good rhythm.
   —George Sarton,
Hellenistic Science and Culture in the Last Three Centuries B.C., 1959

The chart further makes obvious the exact period of days involved in the hebdomadal, post-hebdomadal, and neonatal periods. The first 23 hours and 59 minutes after birth is under one day; an infant has lived 7 full days the moment it becomes 7 days of age; therefore, the correct designation of the hebdomadal period is "under 7 days."
   —Edith Louise Potter and John M. Craig, *Pathology of the Fetus and the Infant*, 1975

hebdomadal

(heb-DOM-ah-dal)

adjective

weekly.

hebdomadism

(HEB-dah-*mad*-iz-em)

noun

a belief that the number seven is sacred.

The Hebdomadal Council was the governing council of Oxford University. It was replaced in 2000 by the University Council.

hebetudinous

(*heb*-i-TYOOD-i-nes)

adjective

dull-minded; mentally lethargic.

"You are a hebetudinous
futilitarian!"
   —Ambrose Bierce,
   "Some Disadvantages of Genius" in *The Collected Works
   of Ambrose Bierce,* 1911

"I've always suspected men like
you wear guns in a futile effort
to disguise your hebetudinous na-
tures. And now I'm sure of it."
   —Joan Johnston,
   Sweetwater Seduction, 1991

hebetude

(HEB-i-*tyood*)

noun

dullness; mental lethargy.

hebetate

(HEB-i-*tate*)

verb

to make dull or obtuse;
to stupefy.

*"This word is striking, bold, and its
meaning is completely unexpected."*

hubris

(HYOO-bris)

noun

excessive pride or self-confi-
dence; arrogance.

To the Greeks, Hubris meant any
kind of overweening and excess.
When men or societies went too
far, either in dominating other
men and societies, or in exploit-
ing the resources of nature to
their own advantage, this overweening exhibition of pride had
to be paid for. In a word, Hubris
invited Nemesis.
   —Aldous Huxley,
   "Idolatry," *Vedanta for the
   Western World*, 1945

hubristic

(hyoo-BRIS-tik)

adjective

"It rolls off the tongue and sounds like a jumble of voices."

hullabaloo

(HUL-ah-bah-*loo*)

noun

loud noise or excitement; disturbance or uproar.

The hullabaloo was caused by the Tululu, a sort of pagan Mardi Gras enjoyed exclusively by masked male dancers who roamed around the huts in bands, snatching anyone they could, beating him with flour sacks and making him dance within the monstrous circle of the Tululu demons.
—Hassoldt Davis,
The Jungle and the Damned, 2000

hypergelast

(hy-PER-ji-*last*)

noun

one who laughs excessively.

The phenomena presented by the misogelast, or laughter-hater; the agelast, or non-laugher; the gelast, who is the laugher himself, and the hypergelast, who is the laugher gone intemperate, are looked into, and as far as possible accounted for, by Dr. Sully.
—Paulist Fathers,
"Views and Reviews," *Catholic World*, 1903

America had become a laughing nation, a country of frivolists and hypergelasts, a culture dangerously out of control.
—Henry Jenkins,
What Made Pistachio Nuts?, 1992

I i

ichthyophagous

(*ik*-thee-OFF-ah-ges)

adjective

eating or subsisting on fish.

It might be inferred from this account, however, that the arts must be in a languishing state amongst a people that did not understand the process of salting fish; and my brother observed derisively, much to my grief, that a wretched ichthyophagous people must make shocking soldiers, weak as water, and liable to be knocked over like ninepins; whereas, in *his* army, not a man ever ate herrings, pilchards, mackerels, or, in fact, condescended to any thing worse than sirloins of beef.
   —Thomas De Quincey,
   "Introduction to the World of Strife," 1861

As these ichthyologists are recognized, the world over, as among the leading ones in America, we cannot do otherwise than follow their lead, although confusion should occur in the minds of knowledge-seeking anglers, who not only delight in artistically killing a surface-rising game fish, but take pride in a knowledge of its rank in ichthyic circles and its scientific as well as common name.
   —William Harris,
   "Our Fresh Water Game Fishes," *Field and Stream*, 1904

ichthyic

(IK-thee-ik)

adjective

of or pertaining to fish; piscine.

ichthyologist

(*ik*-thee-OL-ah-jist)

noun

imbroglio

(im-BROL-yoh)

noun

1. a confusing or complicated situation; embroilment. 2. an intricate plot. 3. a complicated or embarrassing misunderstanding or disagreement. 4. a confused mass.

The Liturgy, or adoptable and generally adopted Set of Prayers and Prayer-Method, was what we can call the Select Adoptabilities, 'Select Beauties' well edited (by Ecumenic Councils and other Useful-Knowledge Societies) from that wide waste imbroglio of Prayers already extant and accumulated, good and bad.
—Thomas Carlyle,
Past and Present, 1893

The show is a comedy of errors and a sex farce rolled up into one cleverly written, laugh-out-loud stage imbroglio of extramarital affairs, would-be affairs and pretend and fake affairs that will have your head spinning.
—Jasmina Wellinghoff,
"Review: 'Don't Dress for Dinner,'" *San Antonio Express-News,* 2008

incondite

(in-KON-dit)

adjective

1. poorly constructed. 2. lacking finish or refinement; unpolished; crude.

I am even prepared to tell my tormentors that perhaps once or twice I had cast an appraiser's cold eye at Charlotte's coral lips and bronze hair and dangerously low neckline, and had vaguely tried to fit her into a plausible daydream. This I confess under torture. Imaginary torture, perhaps, but all the more horrible. I wish I might digress and tell you more of the *pavor nocturnus* that would rack me at night hideously after a chance term had struck me in the random readings of my boyhood, such as *peine forte et dure* (what a Genius of Pain must have invented that!) or the dreadful, mysterious, insidious words "trauma," "traumatic event," and "transom." But my tale is sufficiently incondite already.
—Vladimir Nabakov,
Lolita, 1955

indecorous

(in-DEK-er-es)

adjective

lacking accepted standards of decency or good taste; rude or indelicate.

'Take care, madam!'

'Scrupulous care I will take, Mr. Sympson. Before I marry I am resolved to esteem—to admire—to *love*.'

'Preposterous stuff! indecorous, unwomanly!'

'To love with my whole heart. I know I speak in an unknown tongue; but I feel indifferent whether I am comprehended or not.'

 —Charlotte Brontë,
  Shirley, 1849

In my musings as a naturalist it has occurred to me that while decorum is an excellent thing some must be indecorous if the race is to be carried on since the position prescribed for procreation is indecorous, highly indecorous, and it occurred to me that perhaps that is what these people are, or were; the children of decorous cohabitation.

 —Ernest Hemingway,
  Death in the Afternoon, 1932

Smart combines the forms of litany with indecorous content, confidently associating biblical language and allusions with the personal hygiene of his cat.

 —Robert Pinsky,
  "In Nomine Patris et Felis,"
  Slate, 2009

indecorousness

(in-DEK-er-es-nes)

noun

decorous

(DEK-er-es)

adjective

behaving with decorum; proper or dignified; seemly.

infandous

(in-FAN-des)

adjective

too odious to be expressed; unspeakably horrible.

At the southward there was a beast, which brought forth a creature, which might pretend to something of a humane shape. Now, the people minded that the monster had a blemish in one eye, much like what a profligate fellow in the town was known to have. This fellow was hereupon examined; and upon his examination, confess'd his infandous Bestialities; for which he was deservedly executed.

—Cotton Mather,
Magnalia Christi Americana,
1820

I have seen nothing in the various hypotheses brought forward which did not to me involve a greater improbability than the presumption of guilt. Take that, for instance, that Byron accused himself, through a spirit of perverse vanity, of crimes he had not committed. How preposterous [that] he would stain the name of a sister whom, on the supposition of his innocence, he loved with angelic ardor as well as purity, by associating it with such an infandous accusation!

—Oliver Wendell Holmes,
"Letter to Harriet Beecher Stowe," 1869

Late at night the two youths sat drowsing in their chairs, lulled by the praying of the loom-fixer on the floor below. Gilman listened as he nodded, his preternaturally sharpened hearing seeming to strain for some subtle, dreaded murmur beyond the noises in the ancient house. Unwholesome recollections of things in the *Necronomicon* and the Black Book welled up, and he found himself swaying to infandous rhythms said to pertain to the blackest ceremonies of the Sabbat and to have an origin outside the time and space we comprehend.

—H. P. Lovecraft,
Dreams in the Witch House,
1932

infandum

(in-FAN-dum)

noun

insouciance

(in-SOO-see-ans)

noun

lack of concern; indifference.

Chicago is an extremely cosmopolitan city. Both the Atlantic and Pacific Oceans are hers. The Chicago newspapers advertise, impartially, sailings to Honolulu or Plymouth, to Japan or France. There is a sort of insouciance about it. And also there is insouciance in her evident determination to remain young no matter how the years are piling up. With all the intense absorption in work, there goes also an intense absorption in play; and you will notice such advertisements as that of the "Fisherman's Special," whose times are so arranged as to take Chicagoans, with equipment of dining cars and sleeping cars, from Friday night until Monday, on long trips up among the lakes of Wisconsin.
—Robert Shackleton,
The Book of Chicago, 1920

Fonteyn had an insouciance which allowed her to stray across boundaries and emerge as crisp as royalty itself. She was utterly, even flatly, English, and yet radiantly exotic too; she was virginal, and yet sexually free; bohemian, but

also, as Ashton once remarked, "absolutely bourgeois."
—*The Economist,* 2004

The stranger rode in a bullock-cart, but instead of being seated on the rough cushions therein he stood up like a god, holding on to the rail of the cart's latticework wooden frame with one insouciant hand.
—Salman Rushdie,
The Enchantress of Florence,
2009

insouciant

(in-SOO-see-ant)

adjective

inspissate

(in-SPIS-*ate*)

adjective

thick or dense; inspissated.

Then fell thick night. Inspissate
  darkness reigned
In heaven and earth, and earth shook
  through and through,
Even as the slumbrous silence when a
  hound,
Darkling beside his master's couch at
  night,
Shakes his rough hide like some dull
  cracking thong,
Then settles suddenly in utter sleep.
  —Victor Plarr,
    The Tragedy of Asgard, 1905

inspissate

(in-SPIS-*ate*)

verb

to thicken or cause to thicken,
especially by evaporation.

inspissation

(*in*-spi-SAY-shen)

noun

inspissator

(*in*-spi-SAY-tor)

noun

irenic

(eye-REN-ik)

adjective

promoting peace or conciliation.

As shriller and sometimes hate-
ful voices became identified with
political evangelicalism, Graham
emerged as a more irenic elder
statesman.
    —John G. Turner,
      "Billy Graham, Political
      Operative," *The Christian
      Century,* 2009

irenical

(eye-REN-i-kel)

adjective

jejune

(ji-JOON)

adjective

1. uninteresting; dull. 2. childish;
lacking maturity. 3. lacking in
nutrition; barren.

The putting these glosses on
what they affirm; these, as they
are thought, handsome, easy,
and graceful explications of what
they are discoursing on, is so
much the character of what is
called and esteemed writing well,
that it is very hard to think that
authors will ever be persuaded
to leave what serves so well to
propagate their opinions, and
procure themselves credit in the
world, for a more jejune and dry
way of writing, by keeping to the
same terms precisely annexed to
the same ideas; a sour and blunt
stiffness, tolerable in mathemati-
cians only, who force their way,
and make truth prevail by irresistible demonstration.
  —John Locke,
  *An Essay Concerning Human
  Understanding*, 1823

There, the genuine and whole-
some civilization of the nineteenth
century is curiously confused and
commingled with the Walter Scott
Middle-Age sham civilization; and
so you have practical, common-
sense, progressive ideas and progressive works; mixed up with the
duel, the inflated speech, and the
jejune romanticism of an absurd
past that is dead, and out of charity ought to be buried.
  —Mark Twain,
  Life on the Mississippi, 1883

jejuneness

(ji-JOON-nes)

noun

jeremiah

(*jer*-ah-MY-ah)

noun

1. a Hebrew prophet who is remembered for his lamentations.
2. a person who complains often and sees only a disastrous future.

To some degree a spiritual autobiography, it is also a scathing jeremiad, lighted by flashes of grim humor and noble prophecy, against hollow pretense and false ideals, against the tendency to glorify mechanical progress rather than the things of the spirit.
   —Arthur Lyon Cross,
   A History of England and Greater Britain, 1914

We have had enough, and more than enough, of prophets, revivalists and tragedians. But we have also had enough of the satirists and debunkers, of the writers of farces and the tellers of bawdy stories, to whom long-suffering humanity has turned for an antidote to all those Jeremiahs and Savonarolas, and portentous Dantes, those preachers of crusades and heresy hunters, ancient and modern.
   —Aldous Huxley,
   Adonis and the Alphabet, 1956

Moore's latest nonfiction jeremiad—about the incestuous relationship between government and corporate America—premieres in Los Angeles and New York on Wednesday with the kind of build-up usually reserved for "Spider-Man" sequels.
   —John Horn,
   "'Capitalism: A Love Story' Won't Be a 'Sicko,'" *Los Angeles Times,* 2009

jeremiad

(*jer*-ah-MY-ad)

noun

a bitter lament or prophecy of doom.

junoesque

(*joo*-noh-ESK)

adjective

1. (of a woman) having a stately bearing; regal; statuesque.
2. having the imposing beauty of the goddess Juno.

In spite of this affliction, she looked unusually gay and graceful as she glided away. She seldom ran—it did not suit her style, she thought, for being tall, the stately and Junoesque was more appropriate than the sportive or piquante.
  —Louisa May Alcott,
  Little Women, or *Meg, Jo, Beth and Amy*, 1868

The body types vary too: sapling-slender, thickly muscled, tall, stocky, petite, Junoesque. The ensemble gets its unified look from a common movement style. Each dancer displays the Ailey hallmarks—the powerful, fluent spine, the poised head, the sensitive hands.
  —Tobi Tobias,
  "Visual Inspection," *New York*, 1982

juvenescent

(joo-vah-NES-ent)

adjective

1. becoming young; being youthful. 2. capable of making young or youthful.

The writing is dewlike, everything happens as it really did, with the same juvenescent feel of spring.
  —Allen Ginsberg,
  in a letter to Neal Cassady, 1951

Organizers had crowed happily as they gazed upon the sea of young faces, but could offer the juvenescent crowd only well-intentioned but sad displays of paleofeminism.
  —Rebecca Traister,
  Big Girls Don't Cry, 2010

juvenescence

(*joo*-vah-NES-ence)

noun

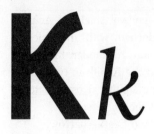

kakistocracy

(*kak*-i-STOK-rah-see)

noun

government by the worst, most unscrupulous, or least qualified citizens.

They had no pamphleteering societies to demonstrate that reading and writing are better than meat and drink; and they were utterly destitute of the blessings of those "schools for all," the house of correction, and the treadmill, wherein the autochthonal justice of our agrestic kakistocracy now castigates the heinous sins which were then committed with impunity, of treading on old footpaths, picking up dead wood, and moving on the face of the earth within the sound and whirr of a partridge.
—Thomas Love Peacock,
The Misfortunes of Elphin,
1829

What fills me with doubt and dismay is the degradation of the moral tone. Is it or is it not a result of Democracy? Is ours a "government of the people by the people for the people," or a Kakistocracy rather, for the benefit of knaves at the cost of fools?
—James Russell Lowell,
"Letter to Joel Benton," 1876

Then in the seventh year of the Reagan kakistocracy, the medical dyes shooting through my arterial freeways were forced to make a detour around a major obstruction.
—John Gregory Dunne,
Harp, 1989

kakistocratical

(kah-*kis*-tah-KRAT-i-kel)

adjective

kosmokrator

(*kos*-moh-KRAY-ter)

noun

ruler of the world.

A Kosmokrator there is, in spite of all our efforts at denial. There is a great and terrible Ruler of the cosmos, who gives forth life, and takes back life. The Kosmokrator gives us fresh life every day. But if we refuse the Almighty, the Ruler, we refuse the life. And whoever cuts us off from the Almighty cuts us off from life. Whoever gets between me and the Lord of Life, the Kosmokrator, Lord of Hosts and giver of might, source of our strength and power and our glory as far as we can be glorious, whoever gets between me and this, or Him, if you like, is my enemy, and hates me.

—D. H. Lawrence,
Apocalypse, 1930

The legendary shield of Achilles was adorned with the celestial signs, and Alexander the Great adopted the Achillean type along with the epithet Kosmokrator—ruler of the universe.

—David Leatherbarrow,
Topographical Stories: Studies in Landscape and Architecture, 2004

L l

"It's just a beautifully sad word. If all the words for despair were this pretty, no one would be sad for long."

lachrymose

(LAK-ri-*mos*)

adjective

1. given to weeping; tearful.
2. causing tears; mournful; sad.

Next morning when she took up the pen to write, either she could think of nothing, and the pen made one large lachrymose blot after another, or it ambled off, more alarmingly still into mellifluous fluencies about early death and corruption, which were worse than no thinking at all.
  —Virginia Woolf, *Orlando: A Biography*, 1928

"You think you've got something to be afraid about?" Doc Daneeka demanded, lifting his delicate immaculate dark head up from his chest to gaze at Yossarian irascibly for a moment with lachrymose eyes. "What about me? My precious medical skills are rusting away here on this lousy island while other doctors are cleaning up."
  —Joseph Heller, *Catch 22*, 1961

lachrymosity

(*lak*-ri-MOS-i-tee)

noun

illacrymable

(il-LAK-ri-mah-ble)

adjective

unable to cry.

"I love the 'softly glowing' sound of this word and all it evokes."

lambent

(LAM-bent)

adjective

1. flickering or glowing lightly.
2. dealing gracefully or brilliantly with a topic. 3. softly bright or luminous.

Notwithstanding, she was proud of him as he lounged in his <u>lambent</u> fashion in her home, he was so attentive and courteous to her mother and to herself all the time. It was wonderful to have his awareness in the room. She felt rich and augmented by it, as if she were the positive attraction and he the flow towards her. And his courtesy and his agreement might be all her mother's, but the <u>lambent</u> flicker of his body was for herself. She held it.

—D. H. Lawrence,
The Rainbow, 1915

lambency

(LAM-ben-see)

noun

laodicean

(ley-*od*-ah-SEE-an)

adjective

1. pertaining to Laodicea or its inhabitants. 2. indifferent or lukewarm, especially about religion or politics.

Once again, we are a kindly people, but we are selfish and callous and incompetent. We are supine and <u>Laodicean</u>. We have a situation before us of revolting ugliness, and yet we do not proceed to alter it.

—Independent Labour Party,
The Socialist Review, 1929

It is thought that the Laodiceans were being criticized for their neutrality or lack of zeal about religion (hence the meaning "lukewarm"). Thus, the term *laodicean* refers to people indifferent to matters of faith or politics. Some scholars, however, have suggested that this metaphor has been drawn from the city's lukewarm water supply. The archaeology shows Laodicea had an aqueduct that probably carried water from hot mineral springs some five miles south, which, before entering the city, would have become tepid.

lascivious

(lah-SIV-ee-es)

adjective

1. given to or expressing lust; lecherous. 2. exciting sexual desires; salacious.

Like every sound and solid citizen, Yuri was an orthodox puritan—not a divine puritan blessed by God with unshakeable principles and austere limitations, but a simple Russian puritan who could not abide spitting in the street, paper on the sidewalk, lascivious dancing, electrified guitars, unhoused female breasts, outlandish clothing, indiscreet language, delicate sauces, Turkish sesame candy, aromatic wines, pictures with flesh tones, photographs of cripples, cripples themselves, expensive cigarettes with gold tips, license, permissiveness, anything which would be considered *"ne kulturny."*
  —Arthur A. Cohen,
  A Hero in His Time, 1976

His eyes, as greasy as his apron, took mocking but lascivious account of her diaphanous dressing gown.
  —Tennessee Williams,
  "Das Wasser Ist Kalt,"
  Collected Stories, 1994

"A simply beautiful and mellifluous word."

lissome

(LIS-um)

adjective

1. lithe or lithesome; flexible; supple. 2. having the ability to move with ease; limber; agile.

O darling Katie Willows, his one child!
A maiden of our century, yet most
  meek;
A daughter of our meadows, yet not
  coarse;
Straight, but as lissome as a hazel
  wand;
Her eyes a bashful azure, and her hair
In gloss and hue the chestnut, when
  the shell
Divides threefold to show the fruit
  within.
  —Alfred Lord Tennyson,
  "The Brook" 1855

I have already lost more than thirty pounds and intend thus to dwindle with dignity until there shall be no other word for me but lissome. Lissome my children and you shall hear ...
  —Alexander Woollcott,
  The Letters of Alexander Woollcott, 1944

"Saying this word slowly really gets the message across. Love it."

loathsome

(LOTH-sum)

adjective

arousing loathing; abhorrent; repulsive; disgusting.

A cry of pain and indignation broke from him. He could see no change, save that in the eyes there was a look of cunning and in the mouth the curved wrinkle of the hypocrite. The thing was still <u>loathsome</u>—more <u>loathsome</u>, if possible, than before—and the scarlet dew that spotted the hand seemed brighter, and more like blood newly spilled.

   —Oscar Wilde,
   The Picture of Dorian Gray,
   1891

"... He preferred the vanity and vexation to the silence and un-movableness of the grave. And so I. To crawl is piggish; but to not crawl, to be as the clod and rock, is <u>loathsome</u> to contemplate. It is <u>loathsome</u> to the life that is in me, the very essence of which is movement, the power of movement, and the consciousness of the power of movement. Life itself is unsatisfaction, but to look ahead to death is greater unsatisfaction."

   —Jack London,
   The Sea Wolf, 1904

loathe

(LOTH)

verb

to abhor; to feel disgust or aversion for.

logogogue

(LOG-oh-gog)

noun

one who issues rules for the use of words.

The contraction is rightly formed, it is easily spelled, it is old in the language, it is even fashionable in certain circles, and it belongs as a brother to *isn't* and *aren't*. Most of all, it is needed. Yet it lies under the damnation of logogogues, though they offer no reason for damning it. It is one of a hundred similar locutions that they have damned without reason.
—Wallace Rice,
"Ain't," *The American Mercury,* 1927

Thus, he implored his readers to beware of logogogues—word tyrants. He warned us to resist the seductive allure of lexographic molesters. Sadly, we have failed to heed that warning. It seems that we are presently witnessing the emergence of our own Newspeak.
—George Grant,
Grand Illusions, 2000

logolatry

(loh-GOL-ah-tree)

noun

1. veneration or worship of words. 2. excessive regard for words.

We are told that the learning of a second and third language, especially if it is a dead language, is a splendid means of cultivating the mind—another superstition, which rests upon no evidence whatever as far as I have been able to ascertain; and we are told that the acquisition of the dead languages is morally and intellectually elevating, a safeguard against materialism, a refining and spiritualizing influence, without which a man remains destitute of all high and worthy motives, sunk in debased and sordid aims and pursuits. I have examined this assertion again and again, and I can find no evidence whatever to support it. It is an assertion as baseless as that the wearing of a charm will ward off misfortune; and the same cast of mind that entertains the one superstition cherishes the other. And the devotion of disproportionate time and attention to languages, whether dead or living, in the scheme of education, is not merely waste; it is actively pernicious and baneful. It does irreparable harm to the growing mind. It fosters and increases that <u>logolatry</u>, that worship of words, that inability to distinguish between words and things, that pseudo-solution of problems by the invention of neat phrases, that pursuit of such flimsy will-o'-the-wisps as socialism, war to end war, destruction of militarism, efficiency, democracy, spiritual influence, and so forth, which to nearly all the people who use them have no clear meaning, but are mere "words of power" like Abracadabra and Ko-gula.

—Charles Mercer,
"Education and the Acquisition of Languages," *Intellect,* 1918

There's one did swear in his sleep, and one cried Murder. Murder equals *redrum*. That's poetic justice. I waste a lot of time in <u>logolatry</u>. I am a verbalist, Cynthia—a tinklin I am the founder and leader of the new school of literature—The Emblemists. I wear a wide black hat, a dirty shirt, boots with spurs, and shave once a month. Traces of egg can be seen at the corners of my mouth. I am hollow-cheeked, exophthalmic, prognathous: I express my views at any and all times, savagely, and with a conscious minimum of tact.

—Conrad Aiken,
Blue Voyage, 1927

logorrhea

(*log*-ah-REE-ah)

noun

excessive, incoherent talkativeness.

The term <u>logorrhea</u> seems intrinsically misogynist, as well as anti-effeminate: for it casts flow as a failure to be masculine. Writing about <u>logorrhea</u>, one wishes to avoid extremes. One wishes simply to list those who have suffered from it, and to note the paradoxes and peculiarities of the affliction. Men who had it: Proust, James, Freud. Whitman had it. Melville had it. So did Coleridge. Trollope had it, feared it, controlled it. Conrad had it; so did Wagner, and Nietzsche. (You begin to see that <u>logorrhea</u> is indistinguishable from genius, creativity, linguistic abundance.) Spenser, Milton, and Wordsworth had it: *The Faerie Queene*, *Paradise Lost*, and *The Prelude* are three masterpieces of <u>logorrhea</u>, of male flow.

—Wayne Koestenbaum,
Cleavage: Essays on Sex, Stars, and Aesthetics, 2000

logorrheic

(*log*-ah-REE-ik)

adjective

"I have loved it since I was a child and my teacher wrote it in my school report. The word sounds as if only the well spoken would be loquacious. The rest of us poor plebs would merely be chatty."

loquacious

(loh-KWA-shes)

adjective

talkative; garrulous.

Twenty words where one would do. Something was wrong with him. He was becoming <u>loquacious</u>. And then I felt a sudden stab of jealousy as I realized that perhaps he too had been affected by the presence of the damsel and was desirous of showing off in her presence.
   —R. K. Narayan,
   The Guide, 1988

loquaciousness

(loh-KWA-shes-nes)

noun

"The very sound of it conjures decadence."

louche

(LOOSH)

adjective

morally dubious; decadent; disreputable.

"Mayn't it have all the air for them of a really equivocal, sinister bargain between us—something quite unholy and <u>louche</u>?"
   —Henry James,
   The Golden Bowl, 1904

The bohemian culture's attraction to absinthe seemed largely to rest on the drink's powerful reputation as a vision-making stimulant. In the hands of bohemian culture, the absinthe ritual took on greater meaning and a refinement in preparation, as if the drinker was somehow readying him- or herself for a greater communion with a higher power. The ritual became known as *la louche.* In French, *louche* means "shady, shifty, seedy, dubious." *C'etait une affaire louche*: It was a shady affair. In English, *louche* means "of questionable taste or morality, shady, disreputable."
   —Deirdre Heekin,
   Libation, A Bitter Alchemy,
   2009

"It brings to mind, Zoltan Karpathy, the Hungarian count from My Fair Lady. *'Oozing charm from every pore, he oiled his way around the floor....'"*

lubricious

(loo-BRISH-es)

adjective

1. having a slippery or oily quality. 2. unstable; shifty or tricky. 3. lewd; wanton; sexually stimulating; salacious.

The purser, who woke quite cheerfully from his sleep (he was lying flat on his back when we entered with a <u>lubricious</u> smile on his face), saved the situation. He said, 'There is no difficulty about Mr Brown leaving, the policeman knows him already. But there is only one solution for Mr Jones. He must leave as a woman.'

—Graham Greene,
The Comedians, 1966

'It is clear you have been a great while at sea, to call those sandy-haired coarse-featured pimply short-necked thick-fingered vulgar-minded <u>lubricious</u> blockheads by such a name. Nymphs, forsooth. If they were nymphs, they must have had their being in a tolerably rank and stagnant pool: the wench on my left had an ill breath, and turning for relief I found her sister had a worse; and the upper garment of neither was free from reproach. ...'

—Patrick O'Brian,
H.M.S. Surprise, 1994

lubriciousness

(loo-BRISH-es-nes)

noun

*"Just say it; hear it in your ears.
It's luscious."*

lugubrious

(loo-GOO-bree-es)
adjective

mournful, dismal, or gloomy, especially to an exaggerated or ludicrous degree.

I have been dreaming that I lived near the Thames—I walked through streets more and more gloomy. I saw <u>lugubrious</u> houses inhabited by <u>lugubrious</u> people, and heard <u>lugubrious</u> discourses. I tried to escape, and found all the streets into which I entered had no outlet. It was always a *cul de sac.*
—John Bowring,
*The Works of Jeremy
Bentham*, 1843

Of course her heart squeaked a bit—she had the same configuration of the lungs as her Uncle Hurlbird. And, in his company, she must have heard a great deal of heart talk from specialists. Anyhow, she and they tied me pretty well down—and Jimmy, of course, that terrible boy—what in the world did she see in him? He was <u>lugubrious</u>, silent, morose. He had no talent as a painter. He

was very sallow and dark, and he never shaved sufficiently.
—Ford Madox Ford,
The Good Soldier, 1915

lugubriousness

(loo-GOO-bree-es-nes)

noun

M

"I love the way this word sounds, and the history of the origin of this word is quite interesting."

machiavellian

(*mak*-ee-ah-VEL-ee-en)

adjective

1. of or relating to Machiavelli or Machiavellianism. 2. cunning, deceitful, self-serving, and scheming.

One thing is clear, however—the Machiavellian side of our brains, where we act out of pure self-interest regardless of the interests of others, is the one that leads us into social dilemmas, while the co-operative, social side provides us with ways to escape from them.
   —Len Fisher,
   Rock, Paper, Scissors: Game Theory in Everyday Life, 2008

Civility, manners, and politeness are fast becoming nostalgic memories, and Machiavellian tendencies are becoming more prevalent.
   —Ed Uyeshima,
   "Travel Etiquette Tips to Avoid Being Taylor Swifted,"
   Examiner, 2009

machiavellian

(*mak*-ee-ah-VEL-ee-en)

noun

machiavellist

(*mak*-ee-ah-VEL-ist)

noun

The Prince (*Il Principe*), a treatise by Niccolò Machiavelli, describes how a prince can either acquire the throne or maintain his reign. Machiavelli wrote that the greatest moral good is a stable state, and that cruelty is warranted if it protects the state.

malapert

(MAL-ah-*pert*)

adjective

impudently bold in speech or behavior; saucy; brazen.

And there is a decencie, that euery speech should be to the appetite and delight, or dignitie of the hearer & not for any respect arrogant or vndutifull, as was that of *Alexander* sent Embassadour from the *Athenians* to th'Emperour *Marcus*, this man seing th'emperour not so attentiue to his tale, as he would haue had him, said by way of interruption, *Caesar* I pray thee giue me better eare, it seemest thou knowest me not, nor from whom I came: the Emperour nothing well liking his bold malapert speech, said: thou art deceyued, for I heare thee and know well inough, that thou art that fine, foolish, curious, sawcie *Alexander* that tendest to nothing but to combe & cury thy haire, to pare thy nailes, to pick thy teeth, and to perfume thy selfe with sweet oyles, that no man may abide the sent of thee. Prowde speeches, and too much finesse and curiousitie is not commendable in an Embassadour. And I haue knowen in my time such of them, as studied more vpon what apparell they should weare, and what countenaunces they should keepe at the times of their audience, then they did vpon th'effect of their errant or commission.
—George Puttenham,
The Arte of English Poesie,
1569

That grotesquely misnamed group, The Responsible Society, has had a bash at the matter, and a group of young members of this thin-lipped sodality has written an open letter to the Secretary of State for Health and Social Services, in which, with the malapert pomposity that marks all puritans, they said to Barbara Castle "We feel that you are unaware that pressures are today being exerted on the personal and emotional lives of young people ..." Having assured themselves a sympathetic hearing with this monumental piece of cheek, addressed to a woman twice their age (even if she doesn't look it) and possessed of 50 times their perspicacity, they went on to deplore the moral turpitude of modern youth ....
—Donald Gould, "Bad Medicine," *New Scientist*, 1974

malapert

(MAL-ah-*pert*)

noun

a malapert person.

maritorious

(mar-i-TOR-ee-es)

adjective

excessively doting on or fond of
one's husband.

MONSIEUR. Still you stand on
  your husband; so doe all
The common sex of you, when
  y'are encounter'd
With one ye cannot fancie: all
  men know
You live in Court here by your
  owne election,
Frequenting all our common
  sports and triumphs,
All the most youthfull company
  of men.
And wherefore doe you this?
  To please your husband?
Tis grosse and fulsome: if your
  husbands pleasure
Be all your object, and you
  ayme at honour
In living close to him, get you
  from Court,
You may have him at home; these common put-ofs
For common women serve: "my
  honour! husband!"
Dames maritorious ne're were
  meritorious:
Speak plaine, and say "I doe
  not like you, sir,

Y'are an ill-favour'd fellow in
  my eye,"
And I am answer'd.
  —George Chapman,
  Bussy D'Ambois, 1607

However, his co-star, Kim Hunter
(who, it is beginning to seem, is
doomed to playing maritorious
and pregnant women for the rest
of her career) has little to do.
  —Bernard Augustine De Voto,
  Saturday Review, 1952

marmoreal

(mar-MOR-ee-el)

adjective

1. resembling or made of marble.
2. hard and white, or cold and reserved, like marble.

Pale, <u>marmoreal</u> Eliot was there last week, like a chapped office boy on a high stool, with a cold in his head, until he warms a little, which he did. 'The critics say I am learned and cold,' he said. 'The truth is I am neither.'
　—Virginia Woolf,
　Diary, 1921

For the woman was Anne Stanton, and this was the house of Governor Stanton, whose face, <u>marmoreal</u> and unperturbed and high, above black square beard and black frock coat, gazed down in the candlelight from the massy gold frame above the fireplace, where his daughter crouched, as though at his feet, rasping a match to light a fire there.
　—Robert Penn Warren, *All the King's Men*, 1946

meacock

(MEE-kok)

noun

an uxorious or effeminate man; a hen-pecked husband.

PETRUCHIO. Be patient, gentlemen; I choose her for myself:
If she and I be pleas'd, what's that to you?
'Tis bargain'd 'twixt us twain, being alone,
That she shall still be curst in company.
I tell you, 'tis incredible to believe
How much she loves me: O! the kindest Kate.
She hung about my neck, and kiss on kiss
She vied so fast, protesting oath on oath,
That in a twink she won me to her love.
O! you are novices: 'tis a world to see,
How tame, when men and women are alone,
A <u>meacock</u> wretch can make the curstest shrew.
　—William Shakespeare, *The Taming of the Shrew*, 1594

VIOLA. See what your patience comes to! Every one saddles you, and rides you; you'll be shortly the common stone-horse of Milan: a woman's well holp'd up with such a meacock. I had rather have a husband that would swaddle me thrice a day, than such a one that will be gull'd twice in half an hour.

—Thomas Middleton,
The Honest Whore, 1604

Wait to be wooed and won. Ay, meacock. Who will woo you? Read the skies. *Autontimorumenos. Bous Stephanoumenos.* Where's your configuration? Stephen, Stephen, cut the bread even.

—James Joyce,
Ulysses, 1937

mediocrist

(MEE-dee-ah-krist)

noun

a person with mediocre abilities and talents.

Of the mediocrist I do not at present speak; but of the dunce, of him whom the ancients would have stigmatized with the epithet Boeotian, and of whom they would have said, rather harshly, that his soul was given him only to preserve, like salt, his body from putrefaction.

—James Ferguson,
The British Essayists, 1823

Years afterward when the chief of the underworld underwent an operation to his head, his active mind returned to a normal condition, and he was a mediocrist.

—Louis Lisemer,
Fate or Destiny? A New Optimism, 1923

mephitic

(mi-FIT-ik)

adjective

1. poisonous; noxious. 2. having a foul odor.

The <u>Mephitic</u> Skunk. It might possibly give the reader some faint conception of the odious character of this creature (for adjectives are weak to describe it) when I say that, in talking to strangers from abroad, I have never thought it necessary to speak of sunstroke, jaguars, or the assassin's knife, but have never omitted to warn them of the skunk, minutely describing its habits and personal appearance.

—William Henry Hudson,
The Naturalist in La Plata,
1903

Still, do-gooder or dilettante, there are at least two things Mrs. McMahon will need to consider as she moves from the forthright sunshine and uplifting narrative of prime-time "sports entertainment" into the <u>mephitic</u> underworld of American politics.

—Jeff MacGregor,
"This Sporting Life: Strange Bedfellows," ESPN.com, 2009

merdivorous

(mur-DIV-er-es)

noun

dung eating; coprophagous.

Its floral odor attracts flies and other <u>merdivorous</u> arthropods, some of which pollinate it. This plant can flower from a corm in a humid atmosphere without soil, and some people grow this species as a curiosity.

—Edward M. Barrows,
Animal Behavior Desk Reference, 2001

Gross is an actor whose success in television has permitted him to assemble the money to make a movie and to surround himself with <u>merdivorous</u> toadies and softly cooing yes-men who spaniel after him all day whispering, "You're a genius, Paul. Really. No, truly, I mean it, dude. Sincerely, you are a god."

—Bill Casselman,
"Thoughts on Remembering War Prompted by Watching the Canadian Film *Passchendaele*," 2008

"This word is both fun to say and interesting in meaning: although it sounds complimentary, it means 'tawdry' or 'prostitute-like.'"

meretricious

(*mer*-i-TRISH-es)

adjective

1. alluring in a gaudy or vulgar way. 2. false or insincere; specious. 3. pertaining to prostitutes or prostitution.

Yet were it so, that these of which I have hitherto spoken, and such like enticing baits, be not sufficient, there be many others, which will of themselves intend this passion of burning lust, amongst which, dancing is none of the least; and it is an engine of such force, I may not omit it. *Incitamentum libidinis*, Petrarch calls it, the spur of lust. "A circle of which the devil himself is the centre. Many women that use it, have come dishonest home, most indifferent, none better." Another terms it "the companion of all filthy delights and enticements, and 'tis not easily told what inconveniences come by it, what scurrile talk, obscene actions," and many times such monstrous gestures, such lascivious motions, such wanton tunes, meretricious kisses, homely embracings

—"(ut Gaditana canoro
Incipiat prurire choro, plausuque
  probatæ
Ad terram tremula descendant clune
  puellæ, itamentum Veneris anguentis)"—

that it will make the spectators mad.

> —Robert Burton,
> *The Anatomy of Melancholy,*
> 1621

He was a son of God—a phrase which, if it means anything, means just that—and he must be about His Father's business, the service of a vast, vulgar, and meretricious beauty.

> —F. Scott Fitzgerald,
> *The Great Gatsby,* 1925

meretriciousness

(*mer*-i-TRISH-es-nes)

noun

"Solves the problem of a polite way to describe 'making water.'"

micturate

(MIK-cha-*rate*)

verb

to eliminate urine; to pee.

"E ... nuff." He paused. "Now that you've managed to somehow <u>micturate</u> on Mr. Muskingum, I can no longer terminate his employment at this time without facing certain legal action. I am therefore forced to have someone for whom I have extreme distrust and dislike under my employ." I said nothing. I made a mental note to look up "<u>micturate</u>" when I got home.

    —Gabe Rotter,
    Duck Duck Wally, 2007

micturition

(*mik*-cha-RISH-en)

noun

minion

(MIN-yen)

noun

1. a servile follower or subordinate, especially one who is fawning. 2. a minor official, deputy, or the like. 3. one who is highly favored; a darling.

LUCETTA. Keep tune there still; so you will sing it out. [*Julia strikes her*] And yet methinks I do not like this tune.

JULIA. You do not?

LUCETTA. No, madam, 'tis too sharp.

JULIA. You, <u>minion</u>, are too saucy.

    —William Shakespeare,
    Two Gentlemen of Verona,
    circa 1590

... Salami insinuated that some justices of the Appeal Court are <u>minions</u> or stooges. A <u>minion</u> is a slave, sycophant, bootlicker, hanger-on, lackey, lickspittle, parasite, yes man, servile or an unimportant person. Those are the kind of people Salami told us adjudicates over cases at the Court of Appeal.

    —Lukman Adeyemo,
    "Judiciary in the Hands of Salami, Others," *Daily Independent*, 2011

miscreant

(MIS-kree-ent)

noun

1. a vicious, depraved, or villainous person. 2. a heretic; an infidel.

"Fitch, sir! don't Fitch me, sir! I wish to be hintimate honly with men of h-honour, not with forgers, sir; not with 'artless <u>miscreants</u>! <u>Miscreants</u>, sir, I repeat; vipers, sir; b-b-b-black-guards, sir!"

"Blackguards, sir!" roared Mr. Brandon, bouncing up; "blackguards, you dirty cockney mountebank! Quit the room, sir, or I'll fling you out of the window!"

"Will you, sir? try, sir; I wish you may get it, sir. I'm a hartist, sir, and as good a man as you. <u>Miscreant</u>, forger, traitor, come on!"
—William Makepeace
Thackeray, *A Shabby Genteel Story,* 1840

miscreant

(MIS-kree-ent)

adjective

misology

(mi-SOL-ah-jee)

noun

hatred of reason, discussion, or argument; hatred of learning or knowledge.

A <u>misologist</u>, he takes ophidian pleasure in the misuse of words, and his sacerdotal gibberish sounds more like the cries of animals than the holy Logos or the alphabet of the god Thoth.
—Edward Dahlberg, *Alms for Oblivion,* 1967

misologist

(mi-SOL-ah-jist)

noun

Coined in 1870, the word *misologist* became popular through Benjamin Jowett's translation of Plato's *Dialogues*: "As there are misanthropists or haters of men, there are also misologists or haters of ideas."

mollycoddle

noun

1. an effeminate man or boy.
2. a person who is overprotected or coddled.

GILBEY. The disgrace of it will kill me. And it will leave a mark on him to the end of his life.

DORA. Not a bit of it. Don't you be afraid: I've educated Bobby a bit: he's not the mollycoddle he was when you had him in hand.

MRS GILBEY. Indeed Bobby is not a mollycoddle. They wanted him to go in for singlestick at the Young Men's Christian Association; but, of course, I couldn't allow that: he might have had his eye knocked out.

—George Bernard Shaw,
Fanny's First Play, 1911

But I knew only too well what a mollycoddle I had made of myself in the estimation of the proper little sportsman on whom I had hoped to model myself. ... "Don't do that; they'll catch him!" ... It was too awful to dwell on. Lord Dumborough would be certain to hear about it, and would think worse of me than ever he did of a keeper who left the earths unstopped. ... And even now some very sporting-looking people were glancing at me and laughing at one another about something. What else could they be laughing about except my mollycoddle remark?

—Siegfried Sassoon,
Memoirs of a Fox-Hunting Man, 1928

mollycoddler

(MOL-ee-*kod*-ler)

noun

mollycoddle

(MOL-ee-kod-el)

verb

to treat indulgently or be overprotective of; to coddle; to pamper.

mucilaginous

(*myoo*-sah-LAJ-ah-nes)

adjective

1. resembling or relating to muci-lage. 2. gluey; sticky; viscid.

Herbert was not mistaken: he broke the stem of a cycas, which was composed of a glandulous tissue, containing a quantity of floury pith, traversed with woody fiber, separated by rings of the same substance, arranged con-centrically. With this fecula was mingled a mucilaginous juice of disagreeable flavor, but which it would be easy to get rid of by pressure. This cellular substance was regular flour of a superior quality, extremely nourishing; its exportation was formerly forbid-den by the Japanese laws.
   —Jules Verne,
   The Mysterious Island, 1874

Removing it is horrible: the roots are a solid mass of squashy, mu-cilaginous nodules like a carpet of slugs.
   —David Stuart,
   "Invasion of the Garden Snatchers," *The Guardian*,
   2008

Apparently, the sheer quantity of sedimented oil, much of it trapped in a slimy mucilaginous matrix, simply overwhelmed and suffo-cated the sea floor microbial colo-nies that normally consume oil.
   —"Oil Spill Update,"
   DeepSeaNews.com, 2011

mucilaginousness

(*myoo*-sah-LAJ-ah-nes-nes)

noun

mucilage

(MYOO-sah-lij)

noun

1. a substance used as an adhesive. 2. a sticky substance secreted by some plants.

muliebrity

(*myoo*-lee-EB-ri-tee)

noun

1. the condition of being a woman; womanhood. 2. the qualities characteristic of being a woman; femininity.

She was certainly handsome; if there was no longer the freshness of youth, there was still the indefinable charm of the woman of thirty, and with it the delicate curves of matured muliebrity and repose.

—Bret Harte, *In a Hollow of the Hills,* 1896

Granted, muliebrity is awkward to pronounce, but the concept shines a light for women seeking to articulate their erotic essence in a single word.

—David Morris Schnarch, *Passionate Marriage,* 1998

muliebral

(*myoo*-lee-EB-ral)

adjective

myriadigamous

(mir-ee-ah-DIG-ah-mes)

adjective

pertaining to someone who marries all kinds.

The truth is that the picture of male carnality that such women conjure up belongs almost wholly to fable, as I have already observed in dealing with the sophistries of Dr. Eliza Burt Gamble, a paralogist on a somewhat higher plane. As they depict him in their fevered treatises on illegitimacy, white-slave trading and *ophthalmia neonatorum,* the average male adult of the Christian and cultured countries leads a life of gaudy lubricity, rolling magnificently from one liaison to another, and with an almost endless queue of ruined milliners, dancers, charwomen, parlourmaids and waitresses behind him, all dying of poison and despair. The life of man, as these furiously envious ones see it, is the life of a leading actor in a boulevard *revue.* He is a polygamous, multigamous, myriadigamous; an insatiable and unconscionable debauche, a monster of promiscuity; prodigiously unfaithful to his wife, and even to his friends' wives; fathomlessly libidinous and superbly happy.

—Henry Louis Mencken, *In Defense of Women,* 1917

"The necro- words seem all to lead into the ultimate ending: necro-biosis, necrolatry, necrology, necrophobia, etc. But this one has a special feel to it because it relates to the future as well as the past."

necromancy

(NEK-roh-*man*-see)

noun

1. communicating with the dead in order to predict the future.
2. black magic; sorcery; witchcraft.

Ah, <u>Necromancy</u> Sweet!
Ah, Wizard erudite!
Teach me the skill,

That I instil the pain
Surgeons assuage in vain,
Nor Herb of all the plain
Can Heal!
   —Emily Dickinson,
   "Ah, Necromancy Sweet!"
circa 1865

"It gives me a thrill whenever I say it, and makes me think of a dash-ingly dark and wicked man with a waxed mustache and black cape."

nefarious

(nah-FAR-ee-es)

adjective

extremely wicked; abominable; villainous.

"I shall be strictly accurate," said Newman. "I won't pretend to know more than I do. At present that's all I know. You've done something regularly <u>nefarious</u>, something that would ruin you if it were known, something that would disgrace the name you're so proud of. I don't know what it is, but I've reason to believe I can find out—though of course I had much rather not. Persist in your present course, however, and I will find out."
   —Henry James,
   The American, 1877

"Think of it! Think of the colossal nerve of the man—the Machiavellian subtlety of his brain. He knew he was going to fail. He knew after two days of financial work—after two days of struggle to offset the providential disaster which upset his nefarious schemes—that he had exhausted every possible resource save one, the city treasury, and that unless he could compel aid there he was going to fail. He already owed the city treasury five hundred thousand dollars. He had already used the city treasurer as a cat's-paw so much, had involved him so deeply, that the latter, because of the staggering size of the debt, was becoming frightened. Did that deter Mr. Cowperwood? Not at all."

—Theodore Dreiser,
The Financier, 1912

nefariousness

(nah-FAR-ee-es-nes)
noun

nepenthe

(ni-PEN-thee)

noun

1. a substance used in ancient times as a remedy for pain or grief. 2. something that induces forgetfulness or eases pain.

Then, methought, the air grew denser, perfumed from an unseen censer Swung by Seraphim whose foot-falls tinkled on the tufted floor.

'Wretch,' I cried, 'thy God hath lent thee—by these angels he has sent thee Respite—respite and nepenthe from thy memories of Lenore!

Quaff, oh quaff this kind nepenthe, and forget this lost Lenore!'
Quoth the raven, 'Nevermore.'

—Edgar Allan Poe,
"The Raven," 1845

Aside from golf and the attendant charity ball, the basic commodity of Palm Springs is its carefully cultivated atmosphere of nepenthean idleness, mostly sun-drenched.

—*Venture*, 1969

nepenthean

(ni-pen-THEE-en)

adjective

> Nepenthe (from Greek, Νηπενθές—*ne penthos*, "not grief, sorrow, mourning") is a medicine that quells sorrow, a "drug of forgetfulness." *Nepenthes pharmakon*, "a drug that chases away sorrow," first appeared in the Fourth book of Homer's *Odyssey*.

"Shining at night. I think it's simply cool."

noctilucous

(*nok*-ti-LYOO-kes)

adjective

shining in the night; phosphorescent.

First, The angels of God have many excellencies, the imitation whereof cannot by men, in this life, be reasonably proposed. The angelical majesty, as a mortal eye would not be able steadily to behold it, much less, in this mortal state may we affect it. A man may not wish to *shine* like Stephen in this world, and have a *face* that may dazzle the spectators. Or, what would it avail, if a man could make a glare on his face, by smearing it with some of the <u>noctilucous</u> invented by the modern chymistry? A *devil* has, before now, pretended unto such a *face*. 'Tis not the face, but the *grace* of an angel, which is here to be aspired after.

—Cotton Mather,
*Magnalia Christi Americana,
Or, The Ecclesiastical History
of New-England*, 1702

nubilous

(NOO-bah-los)

adjective

1. cloudy or foggy. 2. vague or obscure.

Every one cannot learn acting as he can a business. It requires natural endowment, and something of that rare quality which is described by the <u>nubilous</u> epithet of genius. This distinction should entitle the professors to more regard than they often receive, especially as the very faculty which distinguishes them from the common race of man, impels them to imitate, unconsciously, the foibles and the faults of others.

—John Galt,
The Autobiography of John Galt, 1833

He was one of the Bellefleurs who professed to "believe" in God, though the nature of Hiram's God was highly <u>nubilous</u>.

—Joyce Carol Oates,
Bellefleur, 1980

obloquy

(OB-lah-kwee)

noun

1. abusive or defamatory language of a person or thing; calumny. 2. disgrace or bad repute resulting from public condemnation or vilification.

And again, I cannot help but echo, is it unreasonable to ask women to go on, from generation to generation, suffering obloquy and insult first from their brothers and then for their brothers? Is it not both perfectly reasonable and on the whole for their physical, moral, and spiritual welfare?
  —Virginia Woolf,
  Three Guineas, 1938

obloquial

(ah-BLOH-kwee-al)

adjective

obsequious

(ob-SEE-kwee-es)

adjective

1. characterized by servile compliance; fawning. 2. obedient and submissive.

If James had not been proof to all warning, these events would have sufficed to warn him. A few months before this time, the most obsequious of English Parliaments had refused to submit to his pleasure. But the most obsequious of English Parliaments might be regarded as an independent and even as a mutinous assembly when compared with any Parliament that had ever sate in Scotland; and the servile spirit of Scottish Parliaments was always to be found in the highest perfection, extracted and condensed, among the Lords of Articles.
  —Thomas Babington Macaulay,
  The History of England from the Accession of James II, circa 1845

He was not a good designer, but he had connections; he was obsequious to Keating in the office, and Keating was obsequious to him after office hours.
  —Ayn Rand,
  The Fountainhead, 1943

obstreperous

(ob-STREP-er-es)

adjective

1. noisily defiant; unruly. 2. aggressively boisterous; clamorous.

Mamma was an abject slave to their caprices, but Papa was not so easily subjugated, and occasionally afflicted his tender spouse by an attempt at paternal discipline with his <u>obstreperous</u> son. For Demi inherited a trifle of his sire's firmness of character, we won't call it obstinacy, and when he made up his little mind to have or to do anything, all the king's horses and all the king's men could not change that pertinacious little mind.

    —Louisa May Alcott,
    Little Women, 1869

The <u>obstreperous</u> Mr. Stevens fought hard for his state in ways that we have often opposed—to open the Arctic National Wildlife Refuge to oil exploration, to use his perch on the Senate Appropriations Committee to shovel hundreds of millions of dollars in pork projects to the state.

    —*The Washington Post*, 2008

obstreperousness

(ob-STREP-er-es-nes)

noun

obtund

(ob-TUND)

verb

to dull or deaden; to blunt or make less intense.

To conclude: as alcohol, by causing partial paralysis of the nervous mechanism, will sometimes <u>obtund</u> the shock of physical injury, which would otherwise be fatal, so, in like manner, it will deaden the blow of mental pain, which would otherwise destroy the reason.

    —John Charles,
    Habitual Drunkenness and
    Insane Drunkards, 1878

obtundent

(ob-TUND-ent)

adjective

Obtundation refers to impaired mental capacity in a patient, typically one suffering from a trauma or other medical condition. The root word, *obtund*, means "dulled or less sharp."

omphalos

(OM-fah-*los*)

noun

1. a stone believed to mark the center of the world. 2. the navel. 3. the central part or focal point.

—Do you pay rent for this tower?

—Twelve quid, Buck Mulligan said.

—To the secretary of state for war, Stephen added over his shoulder.

They halted while Haines surveyed the tower and said at last:

—Rather bleak in wintertime, I should say. Martello you call it?

—Billy Pitt had them built, Buck Mulligan said, when the French were on the sea. But ours is the OMPHALOS.

   —James Joyce,
   Ulysses, 1937

Delphi was remote but also central. For later Greeks, Delphi was the physical center of the earth, the distances measured by Zeus himself. The omphalos, or "navel," of the earth was located here in the temple of Apollo.

   —Susan Guettel Cole,
   Landscapes, Gender, and Ritual Space, 2004

An omphalos is an ancient stone. In Greek, the word *omphalos* means "navel." According to legend, Zeus sent two eagles to fly across the world to meet at its center, the "navel" of the world. Stones used to mark this point were erected in several areas surrounding the Mediterranean Sea, including at the oracle in Delphi.

"... conjures up chandeliers, velvet and decadence ..."

opulent

(OP-yoo-lent)

adjective

1. having great wealth; affluent.
2. abundant; plentiful.

When, sick of all the sorrow and
    distress
That flourished in the City like foul
    weeds,
I sought blue rivers and green,
    opulent meads,
And leagues of unregarded loneliness
Whereon no foot of man had seemed
    to press,
I did not know how great had been
    my needs,
How wise the woodland's gospels and
    her creeds,
How good her faith to one long
    comfortless.
    —Charles Hanson Towne,
    "The City," 1922

opulence

(OP-yoo-lence)

noun

orotund

(OR-ah-*tund*)

adjective

1. clear, strong, and resonant;
sonorous. 2. pompous, bombastic.

Even the classical-music station
interrupted its third playing of
Ravel's Bolero since Saturday to
announce the homicide in grave
and <u>orotund</u> tones usually reserved for pointing out musico-
logical subtleties.
    —Jake Page,
    The Knotted Strings, 1995

You have said with finality what
needed to be said about the ignorant, misleading, bloated, <u>oro-
tund</u>, bombastic phrase-making of
Edgar and Daley.
    —Bill Sweetland,
    "Education in Chicago: Reason
    to Cheer," *The Huffington
    Post*, 2009

orotundity

(*or*-ah-TUN-di-tee)

noun

ostiary

(OS-tee-*er*-ee)

noun

1. a doorkeeper, especially in a church. 2. someone who guards an entryway; gatekeeper.

---

35. "Beloved, there are seven orders [of men] constituted in the books, for divine service in the churches of God. The first is the Ostiary; the second, the Reader; the third, the Exorcist; the fourth, the Acolite; the fifth, the Subdeacon; the sixth, the Deacon; the seventh, the Presbyter, or Bishop. The Ostiary is the doorkeeper, who keeps the keys of the church."
   —Letter to the editor,
   The Panoplist and Missionary Magazine, 1816

He could watch the doors of the council chamber from there without being close to the disgusting ostiary, who stank of old age and treated him with a signal lack or respect.
   —Dave Duncan,
   The Cursed, 2008

otiose

(OH-shee-*ohs*)

adjective

1. lazy, indolent. 2. useless; pointless. 3. ineffective or futile.

If we work in this way, the equation for demand and supply is otiose—it follows from the rest; and fortunately, too, it is not wanted, because we have determined the whole price system without it.
   —John Maynard Keyes,
   "Alternative Theories of the Rate of Interest," 1937

The amusing paradox with these men of action is that they constantly have to endure long stretches of otiosity that they are unable to fill with anything, lacking as they do the resources of an adventurous mind.
   —Vladimir Nabokov,
   Pale Fire, 1962

otiosity

(*oh*-shee-OS-i-tee)

noun

Pp

paramour

(PAIR-ah-*moor*)

noun

a lover, especially one in a relationship with a married person; an illicit lover.

The seducer appeared with dauntless front, accompanied by his paramour.

—Thomas Babington Macaulay,
The History of England from the Accession of James II, 1914

Rep. Bob Bass said he will introduce a bill in the Texas Legislature to give women the right to shoot their husband's paramours if caught in adultery. Texas law already gives husbands the right to shoot their wife's paramours.

—*Jet*, 1967

"A seemingly nice way to call someone a cheapskate or a tightwad."

parsimonious

(*par*-si-MOH-nee-es)

adjective

excessively sparing or frugal; niggardly; stingy.

Clubs are pleasant resorts in all respects but one. They require ready money, or even worse than that in respect to annual payments—money in advance, and the young baronet had been absolutely forced to restrict himself. He, as a matter of course, out of those to which he had possessed the right of entrance, chose the worst. It was called the Beargarden, and had been lately open with the express view of combining parsimony with profligacy. Clubs were ruined, so said certain young parsimonious profligates, by providing comforts for old fogies who paid little or nothing but their subscriptions, and took out by their mere presence three times as much as they gave.

—Anthony Trollope,
The Way We Live Now, 1875

parsimoniousness

(*par*-si-MOH-nee-es-nes)

noun

patois

(pah-TWAH; PAT-*wah*)

noun

1. a regional, often nonstandard, dialect; uneducated or provincial speech. 2. the characteristic jargon of a group; cant.

Atlanta subdebs have a little pa‐tois somewhat like old Pig Latin which they call *Stinky Pinky*. It contains words like *Super-Snooper* (a G-man), *Flyer-Higher* (an aviator), *Snooty-Beauty* (a debutante), *Hen-Pen* (a girls' school), *Jug-Mug* (a man in jail), and *Silly-Filly* (a young girl).
  —"Subdebs,"
  Life, 1941

—And as I wrote and wrote, I also sought for a way to boil down my argument into the simplest patois of Washington, D.C., the Power‐point presentation.
  —*Daily Kos*, 2009

"This is my new favorite word! I can't believe it's an actual legitimate term."

philander

(fi-LAN-der)

verb

1. to have a sexual, or extramarital, affair with a woman. 2. to engage in many love affairs with women. 3. literary name for a lover.

LADY WISHFORT. What? Then I have been your property, have I? I have been convenient to you, it seems, while you were catering for Mirabell; I have been broker for you? What, have you made a passive bawd of me? This exceeds all precedent. I am brought to fine uses, to become a botcher of second-hand marriages between Abigails and Andrews! I'll couple you. Yes, I'll baste you togeth‐er, you and your Philander. I'll Duke's Place you, as I'm a person. Your turtle is in custody already. You shall coo in the same cage, if there be constable or warrant in the parish.

FOIBLE. Oh, that ever I was born! Oh, that I was ever married! A bride? Ay, I shall be a Bridewell bride. Oh!
  —William Congreve,
  The Way of the World, 1700

But in Archer's little world no one laughed at a wife deceived, and a certain measure of contempt was attached to men who continued their <u>philandering</u> after marriage. In the rotation of crops there was a recognised season for wild oats; but they were not to be sown more than once.

—Edith Wharton,
The Age of Innocence, 1920

philanderer

(fi-LAN-der-er)

noun

"I love this word and its meaning. Just say it, and then read the meaning. I also love the interesting history behind the word."

philippic

(fi-LIP-ik)

noun

1. any of the orations delivered by Demosthenes against Philip of Macedon. 2. any of the orations delivered by Cicero against Antony. 3. a speech characterized by acrimonious, or insulting, language; a tirade.

Instead, he struck out in a fierce <u>philippic</u> against war itself, a practice all too rare these days when government spokesmen on both sides of the Atlantic whitewash the latest Western atrocity, believing the public will accept and indeed welcome the most horrific military action as long as it can be represented as against the terrorist-minded, undemocratic or those seen as a threat to our national interests.

—Hugh O'Shaughnessy,
"Spin-doctors, warfare and what a bullet in the body really does," *Tribune* magazine, June 2009

philogyny

(fi-LOJ-ah-nee)

noun

fondness for, or love of, women.

He was a Turk, the colour of mahogany;
And Laura saw him, and at first was
  glad,
Because the Turks so much admire
  philogyny,
Although their usage of their wives is sad;
'Tis said they use no better than a dog any
Poor woman, whom they purchase like
  a pad:
They have a number, though they ne'er
  exhibit 'em,
Four wives by law, and concubines "ad
  libitum."
  —Lord Byron,
  Beppo, a Venetian Story, 1818

It is a well recognized fact that there have always been, and no doubt will continue to be, a few philogynous men in the service who are prone to contract too many marriages without prior removal of legal impediments to a valid marriage, thereby creating some very involved and complex marital situations.
  —United States Navy,
  The JAG Journal, 1947

philogynist

(fi-LOJ-ah-nist)

noun

philogynous

(fi-LOJ-ah-nes)

adjective

Philogyny, love of women, is the antonym of *misogyny*, hatred of women. *Misandry* is hatred of men.

phlegmatic

(fleg-MAT-ik)

adjective

1. of or relating to phlegm.
2. sluggish; apathetic; unemotional. 3. calm; composed.

Parve lokshn can be compared with the *kalter lung-un-leber*, "the cold lung-and-liver," a person so unflappably <u>phlegmatic</u> as to make any sign of life a welcome relief; Calvin Coolidge in a *kupl.*
 —Michael Wex,
  Born to Kvetch, 2005

Phlegmatic is one of the four temperaments originally defined in ancient Egypt or Mesopotamia. The four temperaments are sanguine, choleric, melancholic, and phlegmatic. A sanguine person has an excess of blood; a choleric person, an excess of yellow bile; a melancholic person, an excess of black bile; and a phlegmatic person, an excess of phlegm. A person's mood or behavior, his temperament, was thought to be determined by how much of each of these body fluids his body held.

platitudinarian

(*plat*-i-*tyood*-ah-NER-ee-an)

noun

a person who frequently utters platitudes.

"You wish me to be complaisant to him?" said Klesmer, rather fiercely.

"I think it is hardly worth your while to be other than civil."

"You find no difficulty in tolerating him, then?—you have a respect for a political <u>platitudinarian</u> as insensible as an ox to everything he can't turn into political capital. You think his monumental obtuseness suited to the dignity of the English gentleman."
 —George Eliot,
  Daniel Deronda, 1876

We have inherited a vast number of social ills which never came from nature. They are the complicated products of all the tinkering, meddling, and blundering of social doctors in the past. These products of social quackery are now buttressed by habit, fashion, prejudice, <u>platitudinarian</u> thinking, and new quackery in political economy and social science.
 —William Graham Sumner,
  *What Social Classes Owe to
  Each Other*, 1883

platypygous

(*pla*-ti-PI-gus)

adjective

having broad buttocks.

In her book on *Les Vénus stéotopygues,* L. Passemard disagreed with Piette on the basis that "these celebrated statuettes called steatopygous are almost all <u>platypygous</u>" (1938, p. 132). In other words, they suffered from an excess of fatty flesh at the sides of their hips, not at the back.
> —Sigfried Giedion,
> *The Eternal Present: The Beginnings of Art,* 1962

plume

(PLOOM)

verb

1. to decorate with feathers. 2. to preen or smooth feathers. 3. to congratulate or take pride in oneself.

My sorrow at parting with Fanny was a proof of the interest she had inspired. It was not her fascination as artist, nor yet her charms of person, that had impressed me; but it was difficult wholly to resist her angelic disposition, upright character, and magnetic manners. Constant association with such a woman was perilous in the extreme; and I could not but rejoice that our familiar relations were broken off, doubtless for ever. I felt that I deserved the approbation of my conscience for not abjuring my steady decorous life for one invested with so much novelty and seduction. There was nothing that prevented me leaping into the giddy vortex of a theatrical career, that I secretly loved, save resolution. I began to <u>plume</u> myself on my strength of will, and was disposed to regard Fate as only another name for weakness and infirmity of purpose.
> —Henry Wikoff,
> *The Reminiscences of an Idler,* 1880

plutogogue

(PLU-toh-*gog*)

noun

1. someone who speaks for, justifies, or advocates the interests of the wealthy. 2. someone who favors wealthy people and tries to defend or glorify them.

—As that man is dangerous who would raise up hate as a champion of his cause, so is that man more dangerous when in the interest of lawless business he suppresses the truth and sneers at those who dare to tell it. The apologies of pious <u>plutogogues</u> (which includes some college presidents) for the lawlessness of plutocrats, whose bounties they have shared, are doing more in this country to inflame the passions of the envious, the ignorant, and debased, and to raise up anarchy than all the sayings of all the demagogues and Emma Goldmans. If the vile monster of anarchy flames and hisses it is largely because of the injustice and evil that men do.

—National Education Association, *Journal of Proceedings and Addresses*, 1909

poetaster

(POH-i-tas-*ter*)

noun

a writer of inferior poetry; rhymester.

At its centre is the wonderful biography of the proud, feckless, bohemian <u>poetaster</u> Richard Savage. A man with whom the younger Johnson had once roamed the streets of London by night, he was an author of high pretensions who believed he was the illegitimate offspring of a great family.

—John Mullan, "Mournful Narratives," *Guardian,* 2009

Coined by Erasmus in 1521, *poetaster* designates an inferior poet. The word was first used in English by Ben Jonson in his 1600 play *Cynthia's Revels;* Jonson then chose it as the title of his play *Poetaster.*

politicaster

(pah-LIT-i-kas-*ter*)

noun

a petty, second-rate politician.

The politicaster needs only to please the majority of the voters, but there is no need to endorse a principle because the only principle that has value for him is the right of those who manage to conquer the plurality of votes. ... The politicaster has no sense of conduct but masters the skills of pleasing the crowds.
—César Caviedes,
The Southern Cone: Realities of the Authoritarian State in South America, 2004

The politicaster is looking for small opportunities—for such pickings and stealings as a careless public may leave for those of his kind. The great politician is looking for great opportunities.
—Samuel McChord Crothers,
"In Praise of Politicians," *The Wall Street Journal,* 2004

prehensile

(pree-HEN-sil)

adjective

1. capable of grasping, especially by wrapping around something. 2. able to grasp, or understand, ideas. 3. greedy; grasping.

Meanwhile Wagner's restlessly prehensile mind was taking up, direct or secondhand, all the notions that the age had to offer.
—Jacques Barzun,
Darwin, Marx, Wagner: Critique of a Heritage, 1941

Animals with prehensile tails include some salamanders; chameleons, and several other lizards; some arboreal snakes; opossums; some phalangers; capuchin, spider, and woolly monkeys; anteaters; pangolins; the kinkajou; various rats and mice; and one porcupine.
—Milton Hildebrand,
G. E. Goslow, *Analysis of Vertebrate Structure*, 2001

prehensility

(*pree*-hen-SIL-i-tee)

noun

prelapsarian

(*pree*-lap-SAR-ee-en)

adjective

1. of or relating to the time before the fall of Adam and Eve. 2. innocent and carefree.

Only celibacy, the renunciation of the very sin that caused the Fall, can restore the prelapsarian integrity; and with the divine gift of free will, "each person should correct his or her own fall" here and now.
> —Helen Rhee,
> *Early Christian Literature*,
> 2005

So those who imagine that Mexico before the coming of the Europeans was some kind of prelapsarian paradise could not be more wrong.
> —Tom Holland,
> "All will be done again as it was in far-off times," *New Statesman*, 2009

"It sounds like something that is the opposite of what it means."

pulchritudinous

(*pul*-kri-TOOD-en-es)

adjective

having great physical beauty; comely.

VIRAG (*Prompts into his ear in a pig's whisper*). Insects of the day spend their brief existence in reiterated coition, lured by the smell of the inferiorly pulchritudinous female possessing extendified pudendal verve in dorsal region. Pretty Poll!
> —James Joyce,
> *Ulysses*, 1937

What I was looking for was a companion—a dazzling, pulchritudinous wench who would hang on my every word and eventually obey my every command.
> —Groucho Marx,
> *Memoirs of a Mangy Lover*,
> 2002

pulchritude

(PUL-kri-*tood*)

noun

quacksalver

(KWAK-*sal*-ver)

noun

one who pretends to having knowledge of medicine, salves, and prescriptions; a charlatan; a quack; a mountebank.

CAP. BOBADIL. Sir, Believe me (upon my Relation) for what I tell you, the World shall not reprove. I have been in the *Indies* (where this Herb grows) where neither myself, nor a dozen Gentlemen more (of my knowledge) have received the taste of any other Nutriment in the World, for the space of one and twenty Weeks, but the Fume of this Simple only. Therefore, it cannot be, but 'tis most Divine. Further, take it in the nature, in the true kind, so it makes an Antidote, that had you taken the most deadly poisonous Plant in all *Italy,* it should expel it, and clarify you, with as much ease as I speak. And for your green Wound, your *Belsamum* and your *St. John's Wort* are all mere Gulleries and Trash to it, especially your *Trinidado;* your *Nicotian* is good too. I could say what I know of the Virtue of it, for the expulsion of Rheums, raw Humours, Crudities, Obstructions, with a thousand of this kind; but I profess myself no Quacksalver. Only thus much; By *Hercules,* I do hold it, and will affirm it (before any Prince in *Europe*) to be the most sovereign and precious Weed that ever the Earth tendered to the use of Man.

ED. KNO'WELL. This Speech would ha' done decently in a Tobacco-trader's Mouth.

   —Ben Jonson,
   Every Man in His Humour,
   1598

quincunx

(KWIN-*kungks*)

noun

an arrangement of five objects in a rectangle, with one at each corner and one in the middle.

The word "quincunx," for which Sir Thomas Browne cherished a love so extreme that he used it in and out of season as though magical virtue lodged in the very sound of it, had not long before been introduced into English use, by the astrologers of the school of William Lilly, from whom Browne doubtless borrowed it. Mr. W. A. Craigie defines a quincunx as an arrangement or disposition of five objects so placed that four occupy the corners, and the fifth the centre of a square or other rectangle. He considers that this sense is due, in its original Latin signification, to the use of five dots or dashes to denote five-twelfths of an as, and he quotes Browne as the first English author to employ it so. But the astrologers used the word to describe a certain aspect of planets, and gardeners a certain arrangement of trees or plants in groups of five. "His quincunx darkens, his espaliers meet," says Pope to Lord Burlington, showing that Villario laid out part of his plantations in sets of five trees each; and Peter-borough helped the poet to do the same at Twickenham. A massing of the quincunx arrangement produces an effect analogous to that of the lines on a chess-board or of lattice-work, while botanists recognise a quincuncial structure in several of the parts of plants. This may serve, perhaps, as enough to lighten with a glimmer the porch of Browne's dark discourse.

—Edmund Goose,
Sir Thomas Browne, 1905

The genteel numbness of Quincunx House—built in 1896 and named after the five cherry trees planted in the walled garden, four in the corners and one in the center—meets the aching memories of another house, the Morning Star, a London establishment, now a condemned empty building, where orphan children were raised and, apparently, prostituted to Sunday visitors called "uncles."

—John Updike,
"Property and Presumption,"
Due Considerations, 2007

quincuncial

(kwin-KUN-shel)

adjective

Originally a Roman coin, the quincunx had a value five-twelfths (*quinque uncia*) of an as, another early Roman coin. On the Roman quincunx, the value was sometimes indicated by a pattern of five dots, though they were not always in a quincuncial pattern.

quotidian

(kwoh-TID-ee-an)

adjective

1. everyday; ordinary. 2. recurring daily.

Dimwitticisms give rise to ineloquence, and it is precisely this that marks so much of our speech and writing. Whatever the occasion, whether celebratory or funereal, quotidian or uncommon, people speak and write the same dimwitted words and phrases. No wonder so many of us feel barren or inconsolable: there are few words that inspire us, few words that move us, few words that thrill or overwhelm us. Persuasion has lost much of its sway, conviction, much of its claim.

> —Robert Hartwell Fiske,
> *The Dimwit's Dictionary*, 2006

Brace yourself for a move away from Lamb's quotidian universe of office girls and landladies and the morning commute. Prepare for an Olympian leap from dewy-eyed sentiment about the aged, and pubescent longing for the girl next door

> —Jonathan Barnes,
> *The Domino Men*, 2008

ragpicker

(RAG-*pik*-er)

noun

one who makes a living by collecting rags and other refuse.

The Ragpicker sits and sorts her rags:
Silk and homespun and threads of gold
She plucks to pieces and marks with
    tags;
And her eyes are ice and her fingers
    cold.

The Ragpicker sits in the back of my
    brain;
Keenly she looks me through and
    through.
One flaming shred I have hidden
    away—
She shall not have my love for you.
    —Frances Shaw,
    "The Ragpicker," 1915

"Like hip-hop mixed with green onions, it just sounds delightful."

rapscallion

(rap-SKAL-yen)

noun

1. a rascal; a scamp; a rogue. 2. a disreputable, dishonest person.

"Got pless my soul! does he think, or conceive, or imagine, that I am a horse, or an ass, or a goat, to trudge backwards and forwards, and upwards and downwards, and by sea and by land, at his will and pleasure? Go your ways, you rapscallion, and tell Dr. Atkins, that I desire and request that he will give a look to the tying man, and order something for him if he be dead or alive, and I will see him take it by and by, when my craving stomach is satisfied, look you."
    —Tobias Smollett,
    The Adventures of Roderick Random, 1748

redoubtable

(ri-DOU-tah-ble)

adjective

1. arousing fear; formidable.
2. commanding respect or reverence; eminent.

To the youth it was an onslaught of <u>redoubtable</u> dragons. He became like the man who lost his legs at the approach of the red and green monster. He waited in a sort of a horrified, listening attitude. He seemed to shut his eyes and wait to be gobbled.
—Stephen Crane,
The Red Badge of Courage, 1895

She had not had the curiosity to follow the reports of the "Ararat Trust Investigation," but once or twice lately she had been surprised by a vague allusion to Elmer Moffatt, as to an erratic financial influence, half ridiculed, yet already half <u>redoubtable</u>. Was it possible that the <u>redoubtable</u> element had prevailed?
—Edith Wharton,
The Custom of the Country, 1913

"It's elegant, avoiding the guttural sound of "disgusting" while preserving the meaning."

repellent (or repellant)

(ri-PEL-ent)

adjective

1. serving to drive away; able to repel. 2. arousing disgust or aversion; repulsive. 3. resistant to something.

I assure you that the most winning woman I ever knew was hanged for poisoning three little children for their insurance-money, and the most <u>repellant</u> man of my acquaintance is a philanthropist who has spent nearly a quarter of a million upon the London poor.
—Sir Arthur Conan Doyle,
Sign of the Four, 1890

He exposed himself as a tongue-tied demagogue whose <u>repellent</u> views on the Holocaust, race and homosexuality are thinly concealed beneath a new Labourish veneer of respectability.
—Iain MacWhirter,
"Griffin Smirks While Real Villains Get Away with Grand Larceny," *The Herald*, 2009

repellent

(ri-PEL-ent)

noun

rhadamanthine

(*rad*-ah-MAN-thin)

adjective

inflexibly and strictly just.

The Consuls had shown themselves no slovens and no sentimentalists. They had shown themselves not very particular, but in one sense very thorough. Rebellion was to be put down swiftly and rigorously, if need were with the hand of Cromwell; at least it was to be put down. And in these unruly islands I was prepared almost to welcome the face of Rhadamanthine severity.

—Robert Louis Stevenson,
Letters from Samoa, 1906

Shocking to report, now past sixty, I still do not know all the words in the English language. The other morning I was reading Owen Chadwick's fine book *Britain and the Vatican during the Second World War* and came upon Chadwick's description of Myron Taylor, President Roosevelt's personal envoy to Pope Pius XII, as 'rhadamanthine.' It bugs me not to know a word. I am content not to know the meaning of the universe, or why God sent sin or suffering into the world, but not to know what a word means is beyond my tolerance. I trust you

will think me on this matter altogether too rhadamanthine, which is to say, severe, or strict, coming from the judge Rhadamanthus in Hades in Greek mythology. But there it is, a tic, and I am stuck with it.

—Joseph Epstein,
"The Pleasures of Reading,"
Narcissus Leaves the Pool, 1999

In Greek mythology, Rhadamanthus, from which the word *rhadamanthine* derives, was a wise king, the son of Zeus and Europa. According to legends, owing to his strict but just integrity, he was made one of the judges of the dead in the underworld.

rodomontade

(*rod*-ah-mon-TADE)

noun

pretentious, self-important boasting or behavior; bluster.

She knows what she's about; but he, poor fool, deludes himself with the notion that she'll make him a good wife, and because she has amused him with some rodomontade about despising rank and wealth in matters of love and marriage, he flatters himself that she's devotedly attached to him; that she will not refuse him for his poverty, and does not court him for his rank, but loves him for himself alone.

—Anne Brontë,
The Tenant of Wildfell Hall,
1848

His big head, his slobbery tongue, his quilted clothes, his rickety legs, his goggle eyes, stood out in grotesque contrast with all that was recalled of Henry or Elizabeth, as his gabble and rodomontade, his want of personal dignity, his coarse buffoonery, his drunkenness, his pedantry, his contemptible cowardice.

—J. R. Green,
A Short History of the English People, 1874

But a blockade against armaments is less warlike than Khrushchev's massive arming of Castro. It is less bellicose than Khrushchev's irresponsible rodomontade of last week, in which he accused the U.S. of plotting an invasion of Cuba and threatened nuclear war. An arms blockade—although it may mean war—is not necessarily a formal act of war, especially if the 139-year-old Monroe Doctrine is interpreted to require it.

—"What Should Monroe Doctrine Mean?" *Life*, 1962

rodomontade

(*rod*-ah-mon-TADE)

adjective

rodomontade

(*rod*-ah-mon-TADE)

verb

S s

sarcophagous

(sar-KOF-ah-gus)

adjective

feeding on flesh, carnivorous.

A witch—and be it remembered that she is always a real woman and not a spiritual or non-human being—goes out on her nightly errand in the form of an invisible double; she can fly through the air and appears as a falling star; she assumes at will the shape of a fire-fly, of a night bird or of a flying-fox; she can hear and smell at enormous distances; she is endowed with sarcophagous propensities, and feeds on corpses.
　—Bronislaw Malinowski,
　　The Sexual Life of Savages in North-Western Melanesia, 1929

sarcophagic

(*sar*-kah-FAJ-ik)

adjective

scatology

(skah-TOL-ah-jee)

noun

1. the study of excrement.
2. a preoccupation with excrement or excretory functions.
3. obscene language or literature, especially that dealing with excrement and excretory functions.

Scatology, however, arguably an even more universal function than sexuality, still retains the power to make us blush, to provoke shame and embarrassment.
　—Jeff Persels and Russell Ganim, *Fecal Matters in Early Modern Literature and Art*, 2004

scatologic

(*skat*-ah-LOG-ik)

adjective

scatological

(*skat*-ah-LOG-i-kel)

adjective

scatologist

(skah-TOL-ah-jist)

noun

scree

(skree)

noun

1. rock debris covering a slope.
2. rubble at the base or the side of a hill or mountain.

Alternate freezing and thawing leaves a legacy of shattered rock debris, and frost-shattered rocks accumulate as scree at the foot of slopes.
　—Kenneth John Gregory,
　The Earth's Natural Forces,
　1990

First, look for the most durable surfaces, such as rock, or vegetation that recovers easily, like grass. Here you can concentrate impact (walk behind one another) without much detriment to the area. In more fragile areas, like scree slopes, spread out as you hike, and step around fragile plant life such as lichen and moss.
　—*Backpacker*, 1999

silentiary

(si-LEN-chee-air-ee)

noun

1. one who observes or recommends silence. 2. an official whose duty is to command silence, as in a court of law. 3. one privy to state secrets and under oath not to reveal them.

The silentiary has four pence of every camlwrw, and of every dirwy, which shall be paid by such as break silence in the court.
　—Howell the Good, "The Privilege of the Silentiary,"
　Ancient Laws and Institutes of Wales, circa 940

The king of the Lazi had been educated in the Christian religion; his mother was the daughter of a senator; during his youth, he had served ten years a silentiary of the Byzantine palace, and the arrears of an unpaid salary were a motive of attachment as well as of complaint.
　—Edward Gibbon,
　The History of the Decline and Fall of the Roman Empire,
　circa 1782

Silentiarius, anglicized as *silentiary*, was the Latin title given to a class of courtiers in the Byzantine court. They were responsible for keeping order and ensuring silence during imperial audiences.

sinecure

(SI-ni-*kyoor*)

noun

a job or position that requires little or no work but provides a salary.

The opposition demanded, as a preliminary article of the treaty, that Pitt should resign the Treasury; and with this demand Pitt steadfastly refused to comply. While the contest was raging, the Clerkship of the Pells, a sinecure place for life, worth three thousand a year, and tenable with a seat in the House of Commons, became vacant. The appointment was with the Chancellor of the Exchequer: nobody doubted that he would appoint himself; and nobody could have blamed him if he had done so: for such sinecure offices had always been defended on the ground that they enabled a few men of eminent abilities and small incomes to live without any profession, and to devote themselves to the service of the state.
    —Thomas Babington
    Macaulay, "William Pitt," 1898

sinecurism

(SI-ni-*kyoor*-iz-em)

noun

"Its sharp sound is perfect accompaniment to its definition. Also, the occurrence of the 'skull' sound adds a hint of malice."

skulk

(SKULK)

verb

1. to lie in hiding, especially for sinister purposes; lurk. 2. to move furtively so as not to be noticed. 3. to evade work or responsibility; malinger.

Most forage rapidly in foliage; some hawk for insects; a few walk on ground or <u>skulk</u> in vegetation; some bob or flick tail; a few fan tail.
　—John Farrand,
　How to Identify Birds, 1988

It appears that they would do almost anything to further their sickening aims. That is why they should not be allowed to <u>skulk</u> in the shadows any longer—they must be held to account for the things they have said and done.
　—Barbara Muldoon,
　"Should this man's views be broadcast into our homes?"
　Belfast Telegraph, 2009

skulk

(SKULK)

noun

a person who skulks.

skulker

(SKULK)

noun

"I love this word because it's a mouthful, but its sounds go together wonderfully."

skullduggery

(skul-DUG-ah-ree)

noun

unscrupulous or deceptive behavior; trickery.

So on the night in question I am standing in the lobby of the Garden with many other citizens, and I am trying to find out if there is any skullduggery doing in connection with the fight, because any time there is any skullduggery doing I love to know it, as it is something worth knowing in case a guy wishes to get a small wager down.
—Damon Runyon,
Money from Home, 1935

soporiferous

(*sop*-ah-RIF-er-es)

adjective

causing sleep or drowsiness; soporific.

One of these, Erdaviraph, a young but holy prelate, received from the hands of his brethren three cups of soporiferous wine. He drank them off, and instantly fell into a long and profound sleep.
—Edward Gibbon,
The History of the Decline and Fall of the Roman Empire,
circa 1782

soporiferousness

(*sop*-ah-RIF-er-es-nes)

noun

sopor

(SOH-per)

noun

a heavy drowsiness or deep sleep.

splenetic

(spli-NET-ik)

adjective

1. of or relating to the spleen.
2. marked by irritability or spite; bad-tempered.

The man, on the contrary, that applies himself to books, or business, contracts a cheerful confidence in all his undertakings, from the daily improvements of his knowledge or fortune, and instead of giving himself up to

'Thick-ey'd musing cursed melancholy,'

has that constant life in his visage and conversation, which the idle splenetic man borrows sometimes from the sun-shine, exercise, or an agreeable friend.
    —Richard Steele,
    The Guardian, 1713

In an age without bylines, it was much easier (and a good deal safer) for 19th-century literary critics to write splenetic reviews.
    —Jonathan Wright, "William Hazlitt: The First Modern Man," *The Independent,* 2008

splenetic

(spli-NET-ik)

noun

a splenetic person.

steatopygian

(stee-*at*-ah-PIJ-ee-en)

adjective

having an excess accumulation of fat on the buttocks.

The biographer's reference harks back to Saartjie Baartman, an African woman known as the "Hottentot Venus" who was exhibited as a "freak" in London in 1810, and was known mainly for the large proportions of her steatopygian buttocks. Galton's initial response as a "scientific man" to this beautiful African woman was that he was "exceeding anxious to obtain accurate measurements of her shape," by which we presume he wanted to measure the size of her buttocks.
    —Lennard J. Davis,
    Obsession: A History, 2008

steatopygic

(stee-at-oh-PIJ-ik)

adjective

steatopygous

(stee-at-oh-PI-ges)

adjective

steatopygia

(stee-*at*-ah-PIJ-ee-ah)

noun

stentorian

(sten-TOR-ee-en)

adjective

extremely loud and powerful.

As the cabriolet drove up to the door, this officer appeared hare-headed on the pavement, crying aloud "Room for the chairman, room for the chairman, if you please!" much to the admiration of the bystanders, who, it is needless to say, had their attention directed to the Anglo-Bengalee Company thenceforth, by that means. Mr. Tigg leaped gracefully out, followed by the Managing Director (who was by this time very distant and respectful), and ascended the stairs, still preceded by the porter: who cried as he went, "By your leave there! byyourleave! The chairman of the Board, Gentle Men!" In like manner, but in a still more <u>stentorian</u> voice, he ushered the chairman through the public office, where some humble clients were transacting business, into an awful chamber, labelled Board-room: the door of which sanctuary immediately closed, and screened the great capitalist from vulgar eyes.

—Charles Dickens,
The Life and Adventures of Martin Chuzzlewit, 1844

This time Milo had gone too far. Bombing his own men and planes was more than even the most phlegmatic observer could stomach, and it looked like the end for him. High-ranking government officials poured in to investigate. Newspapers inveighed against Milo with glaring headlines, and Congressmen denounced the atrocity in <u>stentorian</u> wrath and clamored for punishment.

—Joseph Heller,
Catch-22, 1961

stentor

(STEN-tor)

noun

In Greek mythology, Stentor was a herald of the Greek forces during the Trojan War. His name, from which the word *stentorian* stems, means loud-voiced. Homer said his voice was as loud as that of fifty men together.

struthious

(STROO-thee-es)

adjective

of or relating to an ostrich or a related bird.

Agnew already has added "tomentose" and "struthious" to the national political lexicon. His men are toying with a new word—"spendmanship." And all Agnew has to do is read Mencken, who was known as the sage of Baltimore and thus qualifies as the kind of company the new Agnew rather fancies, and heaven knows what polysyllabic protointellectual fustian he can come up with.

—Hugh Sidey,
"Here Comes the Aggernaut,"
Life, 1970

What did I think of all this? Herr Toppelmann wanted to know.

Frankly?

But of course.

Frankly, I found it struthious. That's S-T-R-U-T-H-I-O-U-S. Of or like an ostrich, of the ostrich tribe. From the Latin *struthio*. From the Greek *strouthos,* sparrow. Out of proportion, but there you are.

—Ivan Vladislavic,
The Restless Supermarket, 2001

subfusc

(sub-FUSK)

adjective

dark or drab in color; dingy; dusky; subfuscous.

"Oh, my dear! She went absolutely potty on some new kind of religion and joined an extraordinary sect somewhere or other where they go about in loin-cloths and have agapemones of nuts and grape-fruit. That is, if you mean Brodribb?"

"Brodribb—I knew it was something like Peabody. Fancy her of all people! So intensely practical and sub-fusc."

—Dorothy Leigh Sayers,
Gaudy Night, 1935

subfusc

(sub-FUSK)

noun

dark, drab clothing.

Subfusc (from Latin for "of a dark or dusky color") refers to the clothes worn at matriculation, examinations, and degree ceremonies at Oxford University. Generally, this means, for men, a dark suit and white shirt, and, for women, a white blouse and black skirt or trousers.

"I find it to be a beautiful word, in the way it looks and sounds, as well as its meaning. It brings me to a place of peace where I can imagine lying in a hammock, shaded by the trees, listening to leaves rustling and the whisper of long grass as it sways in a warm summer breeze."

susurrus

(soo-SUR-es)

noun

a soft whispering or rustling sound; a murmur; a whisper.

The gentle susurrus from the leaves of the trees on shore is very enlivening, as if Nature were freshening, awakening to some enterprise. There is but little wind, but its sound, incessantly stirring the leaves at a little distance along the shore, heard not seen, is very inspiriting. It is like an everlasting dawn or awakening of nature to some great purpose.
    —Henry David Thoreau,
    "A Gentle Susurrus," *Journal,*
    1853

No night bird sang. No dogs barked. No whiff of breeze, no roosting owl, no stalking cat rustled the leaves of any tree. I had gone too far inland to hear the susurration of the sea.
    —Dean Ray Koontz,
    Odd Hours, 2008

susurration

(*soo*-sah-REY-shen)

noun

Tt

tartarean

(tar-TAR-ee-an)

adjective

1. of or relating to Tartarus.
2. infernal; hellish.

It teaches man to be happy when he is sick and afflicted, because such calamities are to be received as demonstrations of God's attention and regard for the individual. It teaches that, any description of organic disturbances may be removed by prayer and supplication; and also teaches the old <u>Tartarean</u> doctrine that, the Supreme Being is angry and vexed perpetually at the majority of mankind.

> —Andrew Jackson Davis,
> *Great Harmonia: The Seer*,
> 1852

From the park path, walk straight to the corner of Burnside and SW Osage Street. Here you stand near what Harvey Scott described in 1890 as the mouth of a "stony canyon whose natural roughness has been aggravated by gravel-diggers. Out of this rises, or did rise King's Greek, a stream of most delicious water, which has now been consigned to more than <u>Tartarean</u> gloom in a sewer." That description sent me to the dictionary; <u>*Tartarean*</u> refers to Tartarus, a sunless abyss below Hades where Zeus imprisoned the Titans.

> —Laura O. Foster,
> *Portland City Walks*, 2008

In classic mythology, Tartarus (from Greek Τάρταρος, "deep place") is a deep, gloomy pit used as a dungeon of torment and suffering that resides beneath the underworld.

tatterdemalion

(*tat*-er-di-MAL-yen)

noun

a ragamuffin.

LADY WISHFORT. Will Sir Rowland be here, say'st thou? When, Foible?

FOIBLE. Incontinently, madam. No new sheriff's wife expects the return of her husband after knighthood with that impatience in which Sir Rowland burns for the dear hour of kissing your ladyship's hand after dinner.

LADY WISHFORT. Frippery? Superannuated frippery? I'll frippery the villain; I'll reduce him to frippery and rags, a <u>tatterdemalion</u>!—I hope to see him hung with tatters, like a Long Lane pent-house, or a gibbet thief. A slander-mouthed railer! I warrant the spendthrift prodigal's in debt as much as the million lottery, or the whole court upon a birthday. I'll spoil his credit with his tailor. Yes, he shall have my niece with her fortune, he shall.

—William Congreve,
The Way of the World, 1700

tenebrous

(TEN-ah-bres)

adjective

1. gloomy; dark. 2. obscure; murky.

It is strange how I accepted this unforeseen partnership, this choice of nightmares forced upon me in the <u>tenebrous</u> land invaded by these mean and greedy phantoms.
    —Joseph Conrad,
    Heart of Darkness, 1899

So forget the stripped altars and pared down practices of our British traditions. Imagine clouds of incense in <u>tenebrous</u> Baroque churches. Here are statues of saints at their agonised devotions, grisly Christ figures dripping blood; here are weeping virgins and excruciated martyrs, penitent Magdalenes and venerable nuns.
    —Rachel Campbell-Johnston,
    "The Sacred Made Real at the National Gallery," *The Times*, 2009

tenebrific

(*ten*-ah-BRIF-ik)

adjective

tenebrious

(tah-NEE-bri-es)

adjective

tergiversator

(TER-ji-ver-*sey*-tor)

noun

1. someone who speaks or acts evasively or equivocally.
2. someone who changes sides; an apostate; a renegade.

But when urged by others, I have never conceived that having been in public life requires me to belie my sentiments, or even to conceal them. When I am led by conversation to express them, I do it with the same independence here which I have practiced everywhere, and which is inseparable from my nature. But enough of this miserable tergiversator, who ought indeed either to have been more of truth, or less trusted by his country.

—Thomas Jefferson,
"Letter to George Washington," 1796

Yet even to such a one, notwithstanding his horror of the *ficum voco ficum* buckram and swashbuckler, comes the one clear cry and earnest recommendation to spigot the faucet and throttle the cock, the cockwash, and cut the cackle. This tergiversator lends ear in accordance, and with the terrible scowl, with the very worse will in the world, he drags

himself across the threshold of the gehenna of narration recta.

—Samuel Beckett,
Dream of Fair to Middling Women, 1932

tergiversate

(TER-ji-ver-*sate*)

verb

tergiversation

(*TER*-ji-ver-*sey*-shen)

noun

tergiversatory

(ter-ji-VER-*sah*-tor-ee)

adjective

"The word is rhythmic and naturally descends in pitch as you say it. It's a musical word."

tintinnabulation

(*tin*-ti-*nab*-yah-LEY-shen)

noun

1. the ringing or tinkling sound of bells. 2. a ringing or tinkling that sounds like bells.

Hear the sledges with the bells
Silver bells!
What a world of merriment their
melody foretells!
How they tinkle, tinkle, tinkle,
In the icy air of night!
While the stars that oversprinkle
All the heavens, seem to twinkle
With a crystalline delight;
Keeping time, time, time,
In a sort of Runic rhyme,
To the tintinnabulation that so
   musically wells
From the bells, bells, bells, bells,
Bells, bells, bells
From the jingling and the tinkling of
   the bells.
   —Edgar Allan Poe,
   "The Bells," 1848

The auction dinner this year will be prepared by six outstanding chefs from across the country. ... The collective tintinnabulation of pots and pans and the whisking of exotic sauces should produce a din of gastronomic chamber music in the food preparation tent.
   —George Starke,
   "Up and Down the Wine
   Roads," *St. Helena Star,* 2009

tintinnabulum

(*tin*-ti-NAB-yah-lum)

noun

a small, tinkling bell.

"I love this word because once you hear it you become addicted to telling everyone what it means."

tittle

(TIT-el)

noun

1. a small diacritic mark, such as an accent over an *e* or dot over an *i*. 2. a tiny amount; a jot or whit.

It was evident from the opening sortie that Mr. Justice Cornfield meant to see justice done—to Mr. Conklin Cliffstatter, who sat bored among his attorneys and seemed not to care a tittle whether justice were done or not.
—Ellery Queen,
There Was an Old Woman,
1943

Ellery Queen is both the name of the fictional detective and the pseudonym of the authors of the series, cousins Daniel Nathan and Manford Lepofsky.

troglodyte

(TROG-lah-*dite*)

noun

1. a member of a prehistoric race that lived in caves; a person who lives in a cave. 2. a recluse. 3. a reactionary, brutish person. 4. an anthropoid ape.

God bless me, the man seems hardly human! Something troglodytic, shall we say? or can it be the old story of Dr. Fell? or is it the mere radiance of a foul soul that thus transpires through, and transfigures, its clay continent?
—Robert Louis Stevenson,
The Strange Case of Dr. Jekyll and Mr. Hyde, 1886

The outspoken lady had called him a troglodyte, which had greatly shocked the polite company; most of them didn't know what the word meant, but when they learned that it was a cave-dweller, they didn't think any better of the manners of Miss Creston.
—Upton Sinclair,
Dragon Harvest, 1945

troglodytic

(*trog*-lah-DIT-ik)

adjective

truculent

(TRUK-yah-lent)

adjective

1. aggressively hostile; pugnacious. 2. harsh; scathing.

Only the negro and I were near enough to hear what he said, but the policeman caught something in the tone and looked over with truculent eyes.

"What's all this?" he demanded.
  —F. Scott Fitzgerald,
  The Great Gatsby, 1925

truculence

(TRUK-yah-lence)

noun

turpitude

(TUR-pi-*tood*)

noun

depravity; degenerate or base behavior; wickedness.

The ultimate Author of all our volitions is the Creator of the world, who first bestowed motion on this immense machine, and placed all beings in that particular position, whence every subsequent event, by an inevitable necessity, must result. Human actions, therefore, either can have no moral turpitude at all, as proceeding from so good a cause; or if they have any turpitude, they must involve our Creator in the same guilt, while he is acknowledged to be their ultimate cause and author.
  —David Hume,
  An Enquiry Concerning Human Understanding, 1748

Uu

uberous

(OO-ber-es)

adjective

1. plentiful; fertile; abundant; bountiful. 2. supplying abundant nourishment.

Is it a young and comely peasant-nurse
That poseth? (be the phrase accorded me!)
Each feminine delight of florid lip,
Eyes brimming o'er and brow bowed down with love,
Marmoreal neck and bosom
  uberous,—
Glad on the paper in a trice they go
To help his notion of the Mother-Maid:
  —Robert Browning,
  The Ring and the Book, 1868

"It's slick, oily (like a used car salesman)."

unctuous

(UNK-choo-es)

adjective

1. characterized by affected, exaggerated, or insincere earnestness; obsequious. 2. resembling or having the characteristics of oil, ointment, fat, or grease; oily; greasy. 3. rich in organic matter; soft and smooth.

These were, an internal wooden coffin, very much decayed, and the body carefully wrapped in cerecloth, into the folds of which a quantity of unctuous or greasy matter, mixed with resin, as it seemed, had been melted, so as to exclude as effectually as possible the external air.
  —Edmund Burke (editor),
  The Annual Register, 1823

Owing, however, to a somewhat massive accumulation of animal substance about the lower region of his face, the look was, perhaps, unctuous, rather than spiritual, and had, so to speak, a kind of fleshy effulgence, not altogether so satisfactory as he doubtless intended it to be.
  —Nathaniel Hawthorne,
  The House of Seven Gables, 1851

Last week, 72-year-old Republican and decorated war veteran John McCain appeared on The Late Show, having choppered in so as not to twice disappoint the <u>unctuous</u> David Letterman, who demanded an on-air apology and who got one as McCain, the man who would be president, genuflected before a man whose claim to fame is a lame Top 10 list.

—Shelley Fralic,
Vancouver Sun, 2008

unctuousness

(UNK-choo-es-nes)

noun

unctuosity

(*unk*-choo-OS-i-tee)

noun

unction

(UNGK-shen)

noun

untune

(un-TOON)

verb

1. to discompose; to upset.
2. cause to be out of tune.

A celebrated musician was wont to say, that men knew not how much more he delighted himself with his playing than he did others; for if they knew, his hearers would rather demand of him than give him a reward. The scholar is here to fill others with love and courage by confirming their trust in the love and wisdom which are at the heart of all things; to affirm noble sentiments; to hear them wherever spoken, out of the deeps of ages, out of the obscurities of barbarous life, and to republish them: —to <u>untune</u> nobody, but to draw all men after the truth, and to keep men spiritual and sweet.

—Ralph Waldo Emerson,
"The Scholar," 1876

uxorious

(uk-SOR-ee-es)

adjective

excessively doting on or submissive to one's wife; philogyny.

'Tis a great fault (for some men are <u>uxorious</u>) to be too fond of their wives, to dote on them as Senior Deliro on his Fallace, to be too effeminate, or as some do, to be sick for their wives, breed children for them, and like the Tiberini lie in for them, as some birds hatch eggs by turns, they all do women's offices: Caelius Rhodiginus makes mention of a fellow out of Seneca, that was so besotted on his wife, he could not endure a moment out of her company, he wore her scarf when he went abroad next his heart, and would never drink but in that cup she began first.
— Robert Burton,
The Anatomy of Melancholy,
1621

In many ways he is the antithesis of the traditional footballer: a family man, <u>uxorious</u> to the extent of accepting a public pussy-whipping, and he prides himself on the sexual ambiguity of his image.
— Simon Barnes,
"Ten Athletes Who Changed Our View of Sport," *Times Online*, 2008

uxoriousness

(uk-SOR-ee-es-nes)

noun

A related word is *uxoricide* (from Latin *uxor*, "wife"), the murder of one's wife. *Uxoricide* refers to the murder or the murderer.

"I have not yet found a doctor who can define the word."

valetudinarian

(*val*-i-*tood*-en-AR-ee-an)

noun

a person who is excessively and morbidly concerned with his or her health.

And, Sir, he is a valetudinarian, one of those who are always mending themselves. I do not know a more disagreeable character than a valetudinarian, who thinks he may do any thing that is for his ease, and indulges himself in the grossest freedoms.
—James Boswell,
The Life of Samuel Johnson, 1791

Mr. Welland, in particular, had the privilege of attracting her notice. Of her sons-in-law he was the one she had most consistently ignored; and all his wife's efforts to represent him as a man of forceful character and marked intellectual ability (if he had only "chosen") had been met with a derisive chuckle. But his eminence as a valetudinarian now made him an object of engrossing interest, and Mrs. Mingott issued an imperial summons to him to come and compare diets as soon as his temperature permitted; for old Catherine was now the first to recognise that one could not be too careful about temperatures.
—Edith Wharton,
The Age of Innocence, 1920

valetudinarian

(*val*-i-*tood*-en-AR-ee-an)

adjective

1. chronically ill; sickly. 2. excessively and morbidly concerned with one's health.

valetudinarianism

(*val*-i-*too*-di-NAR-ee-an-iz-em)

noun

"What a fantastic insult!"

virago

(vah-RAH-go)

noun

1. a noisy, scolding, ill-tempered woman; termagant. 2. a large, strong, courageous woman.

Company at dinner, Trench (Ford A's brother), Hardman & his daughter, and two more <u>viraginous</u> old spinsters & Blues (whose names I forget) neighbours of my Lords.

　—Thomas Moore,
　The Journal of Thomas Moore,
　1821–1825

I want to thank you for calling attention to the rhetoric that has changed me from a "sweet," "dear" little old lady into a fierce, cranky <u>virago</u>.

　—Constance Kelly,
　in a letter to the *New York Times*, 2008

viraginous

(vah-RAJ-i-nes)

adjective

From the same root as the word *virile* (Latin *vir*, "man"), virago is a masculine woman. In earlier times, considered a scold or termagant, a virago was often punished with cucking, or being dunked in water. Though used to disparage women who act aggressively, the word *virago* also has a favorable denotation: a courageous, brave woman.

vulgarian

(vul-GAR-ee-an)

noun

1. a vulgar, unrefined person.
2. a person who makes a display of his wealth or position.

"Hopeless <u>vulgarian</u>!" exclaimed Cecil, almost before they were out of earshot.

"Oh, Cecil!"

"I can't help it. It would be wrong not to loathe that man."

"He isn't clever, but really he is nice."

"No, Lucy, he stands for all that is bad in country life. In London he would keep his place. He would belong to a brainless club, and his wife would give brainless dinner parties. But down here he acts the little god with his gentility, and his patronage, and his sham aesthetics, and every one—even your mother—is taken in."

—E. M. Forster,
A Room with a View, 1908

A philistine is a full-grown person whose interests are of a material and commonplace nature, and whose mentality is formed of the stock ideas and conventional ideals of his or her group and time. I have said "full-grown person" because the child or the adolescent who may look like a small philistine is only a small parrot mimicking the ways of confirmed <u>vulgarians</u>, and it is easier to be a parrot than to be a white heron. "<u>Vulgarian</u>" is more or less synonymous with "philistine": the stress in a <u>vulgarian</u> is not so much on the conventionalism of a philistine as on the vulgarity of some of his conventional notions.

—Vladimir Nabokov,
"Philistines and Philistinism,"
Lectures on Russian Literature,
1981

Ww

wheyface

(WEY-*face*)

noun

a person with a pallid face.

How can one laugh after all the misery they've poisoned us with, the whey-faced, lantern-jawed, sad, suffering, solemn, serious, seraphic spirits? I understand the treachery that inspired them. I forgive them their genius. But it's hard to free oneself from all the sorrow they've created.
—Henry Miller,
Black Spring, 1936

I have no use for whey-faced widows or limp-boned virgins.
—Renee Bernard,
A Lady's Pleasure, 2006

whey-faced

(WEY-*faced*)

adjective

witling

(WIT-ling)

noun

1. a would-be wit. 2. a person of scant wit.

While through the press enraged
    Thalestris flies,
And scatters death around from both
    her eyes;
A beau and witling perish'd in the
    throng;
One died in metaphor, and one in
    song.
'O cruel nymph! a living death I
    bear,'
Cried Dapperwit, and sunk beside
    his chair.
A mournful glance Sir Fopling up
    wards cast,
'Those eyes are made so killing!' —
    was his last.
Thus on Meander's flowery margin
    lies
The expiring swan, and as he sings,
    he dies!
—Alexander Pope,
The Rape of the Lock, 1712

wittol

(WIT-el)

noun

a man who is aware of and puts up with his wife's infidelity; a complacent cuckold.

FORD. What a damn'd Epicurean rascal is this! My heart is ready to crack with impatience. Who says this is improvident jealousy? My wife hath sent to him; the hour is fix'd; the match is made. Would any man have thought this? See the hell of having a false woman! My bed shall be abus'd, my coffers ransack'd, my reputation gnawn at; and I shall not only receive this villainous wrong, but stand under the adoption of abominable terms, and by him that does me this wrong. Terms! names! Amaimon sounds well; Lucifer, well; Barbason, well; yet they are devils' additions, the names of fiends. But cuckold! Wittol! Cuckold! the devil himself hath not such a name. Page is an ass, a secure ass; he will trust his wife; he will not be jealous; I will rather trust a Fleming with my butter, Parson Hugh the Welshman with my cheese, an Irishman with my aqua-vitae bottle, or a thief to walk my ambling gelding, than my wife with herself. Then she plots, then she ruminates, then she devises; and what they think in their hearts they may effect, they will break their hearts but they will effect. God be prais'd for my jealousy! Eleven o'clock the hour. I will prevent this, detect my wife, be reveng'd on Falstaff, and laugh at Page. I will about it; better three hours too soon than a minute too late. Fie, fie, fie! cuckold! cuckold! cuckold!

—William Shakespeare,
The Merry Wives of Windsor,
1601

Yet "Bewitched" the television series did as much as anything in American popular culture to alter these archaic assumptions about marriage. Samantha never really sacrificed her powers for Darren and domesticity, and the poor chump himself could hardly have been unaware of the fact. He was a pathetic wittol in the case of his wife's infidelity with the always comic dark powers.

—James Bowman,
"Ditz of the Dark Arts,"
New York Sun, 2005

womanfully

(WOOM-an-*ful*-ee)

adverb

in the manner or spirit of a woman.

She manfully struggled on, however—<u>womanfully</u> would perhaps be a stronger and more appropriate word. She had to calculate not only how to play her own hand correctly, but she had to calculate on her partner's probable errors.

—Anthony Trollope,
The Bertrams, 1859

The part suits Miss Thorndike really well, is neither too sweet nor too melancholy, and permits just that dash of astringency which is her greatest asset. Katharine had both spirit and character, and bore her woes <u>womanfully</u>.

—James Agate,
"The Comedy of Errors," *Brief Chronicles,* 1972

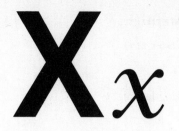

xanthodontous

(*zan*-thoh-DON-tus)

adjective

having yellow teeth.

That I am becoming, or have become, xanthodontous cannot be
of interest to anybody.
  —James Agate,
  Ego 9: Concluding the Autobi-
  ography of James Agate, 1948

Now you know what to tell that
"sweet young thing" who wants
beautiful white teeth. Just tell her
that she is naturally xanthodontous. It will not make her teeth
any whiter, but it will exalt her
ego. Who could be xanthodontous
and not be happy!
  —Michigan Dental Association, 1951

Yy

yesternight

(YES-ter-*nite*)

adverb

during last night.

"*I love this word because it follows seamlessly from 'yesterday.' I first heard the word from my daughter when she was about four years old. In her mind, the transition was a natural flow from 'yesterday.'*"

yesternight

(YES-ter-*nite*)

noun

last night.

'I disturbed nobody, Nelly,' he replied; 'and I gave some ease to myself. I shall be a great deal more comfortable now; and you'll have a better chance of keeping me underground, when I get there. Disturbed her? No! she has disturbed me, night and day, through eighteen years—incessantly—remorselessly—till <u>yesternight</u>; and <u>yesternight</u> I was tranquil. I dreamt I was sleeping the last sleep by that sleeper, with my heart stopped and my cheek frozen against hers.'
   —Emily Brontë,
   Wuthering Heights, 1847

Z z

zygal

(ZI-gel)

adjective

relating to or shaped like a yoke; having a shape like the letter H.

Zachary, a zingaro of Zinder, in the Sudan, was a Zouave, a fighter of renown against Zulus, zaptichs, and other savage tribes; and a <u>zygal</u>—H-shaped—wound on his left zygoma (commonly known as "cheek-bone") honoured and rather improved his manly features.
—*Punch,* 1936

The
BEST WORDS
Quizzes

Quiz 1

1. logorrhea
a. loss of property of a person outlawed or sentenced to die.
b. 1. a class of serfs in ancient Sparta. 2. a serf or slave.
c. littleness of mind; meanness.
d. excessive talkativeness.

2. botryoidal
a. 1. coming before; preceding. 2. anticipatory.
b. shaped like a bunch of grapes.
c. of or like Boeotia or its people; dull and stupid.
d. shaped like a coin; oval.

3. frippery
a. the higher division of the seven liberal arts in the Middle Ages, composed of geometry, astronomy, arithmetic, and music.
b. extremely loud.
c. 1. pretentious, showy finery. 2. something trivial or nonessential.
d. 1. the state of being casually dressed. 2. casual attire. 3. a careless manner.

4. benighted
a. 1. productive of offspring or vegetation; fruitful. 2. intellectually productive.
b. 1. unenlightened; morally or intellectually ignorant. 2. overtaken by darkness.
c. wishing evil or harm to others; malicious.
d. shining brilliantly; resplendent.

5. mucilaginous
a. 1. having or covered with small scales or projections. 2. difficult, knotty. 3. dealing with indecent themes.
b. having the shape of the head of an ax.
c. 1. resembling mucilage; slimy and sticky. 2. producing or secreting mucilage.
d. being or seeming to be everywhere at the same time; omnipresent.

6. cotquean
a. a petty writer; an indifferent author.
b. 1. a coarse, masculine woman. 2. a man who does work regarded as suitable only to women.
c. 1. bearing or manner. 2. an appearance or aspect.
d. 1. wealth; money. 2. the personification of wealth and of inordinate desire for it.

7. cockalorum
a. 1. a conceited, self-important little man.
b. 1. wide-ranging; universality. 2. broad-mindedness; inclusiveness.
c. the study of oneself.
d. a philosophy of the world or of human life.

8. gehenna
a. In Islam, the crier who calls the faithful to prayer.
b. 1. a place or state of torment or suffering. 2. hell.
c. military materiel, such as weapons and ammunition.
d. a body opening or passage, such as the opening of the ear.

9. quacksalver
a. one who makes a living scavenging rags and refuse.
b. the study of miracles.
c. 1. a heroic champion. 2. a strong defender of a cause.
d. a charlatan.

10. deliquesce
a. 1. to melt away; to disappear as if by melting. 2. to dissolve.
b. to ascribe material existence to.
c. to behead.
d. to grow abnormally large.

11. miscreant
a. 1. a drug believed to cause forgetfulness of sorrow. 2. something that causes forgetfulness.
b. something that has the appearance of being true or real.
c. 1. an evildoer; a villain. 2. an infidel; a heretic.
d. 1. a list of people who have died. 2. an obituary.

12. bibulous
a. fruitless; futile; useless; without benefit; unprofitable.
b. 1. morally neutral or indifferent. 2. neither harmful nor helpful.
c. resolutely courageous; fearless.
d. 1. absorbent. 2. addicted to or fond of alcoholic beverages.

13. anfractuous
a. full of twists and turns; tortuous.
b. having given birth two or more times.
c. 1. easily bent; supple. 2. having the ability to move with ease.
d. having no teeth; toothless.

14. quincunx
a. government by the masses; mob rule.
b. a person who lives in seclusion for religious reasons; a hermit.
c. five objects in a rectangle, with one at each corner and one in the middle.
d. an aversion to food.

15. apollonian
a. having the power to cure; healing or restorative.
b. characterized by clarity, harmony, and restraint; serene.
c. of, relating to, or supported by charity.
d. incapable or being mixed or blended.

16. rodomontade
a. 1. a flight to escape danger. 2. the flight of Muhammad from Mecca to Medina.
b. one who believes that human endeavor is futile.
c. a vulgar person, especially one who makes a display of his money.
d. pretentious boasting or bragging; bluster.

17. wittol
a. a woman regarded as disreputable; a prostitute.
b. 1. a coarse sturdy cloth made of cotton and flax. 2 pretentious speech or writing.
c. a man who tolerates his wife's infidelity.
d. a washing or cleansing of the body.

18. abstemious
a. unfamiliar with mathematical concepts and methods.
b. 1. gloomy and dark; infernal; hellish. 2. of or relating to the river Styx.
c. of, relating to, or filled with passion.
d. eating and drinking in moderation.

19. plume
a. to pride or congratulate (oneself).
b. to bend or curve; wind.
c. to confine within walls; imprison.
d. to go to or live in the country.

20. philippic
a. 1. one who seeks to overthrow popular ideas. 2. one who destroys sacred religious images.
b. a harsh often insulting verbal denunciation; a tirade.
c. a concept affirming the independent nature of Black culture.
d. a very small quantity; jot.

21. tartarean
a. of or provoking controversy or given to specious reasoning.
b. infernal; hellish.
c. 1. coming before; preceding. 2. expectant; anticipatory.
d. 1. morally neutral or indifferent. 2. neither harmful nor helpful.

22. babylonian
a. relating to medicine or a physician.
b. of or relating to a sheriff.
c. of or relating to leaping or dancing.
d. excessively luxurious, pleasure seeking, or wicked.

23. rapscallion
a. a person devoted to the study or writing of literature.
b. a rascal; rogue.
c. someone who studies political elections.
d. an establishment for study and learning.

24. dicephalous
a. having two heads.
b. living in mud.
c. having a finely scalloped or wavy edge.
d. feeding on grain or seeds.

25. inspissate
a. 1. to penalize by fining. 2. to acquire by trickery or deception.
b. to cause consternation in.
c. to undergo thickening or cause to thicken.
d. to view with contempt.

Answers to Quiz 1
1. d 2. b 3. c 4. b 5. c
6. b 7. a 8. b 9. d 10. a
11. c 12. d 13. a 14. c 15. b
16. d 17. c 18. d 19. a 20. b
21. b 22. d 23. b 24. a 25. c

Q*uiz 2*

26. juvenescent
a. providing introductory instruction.
b. barefoot or wearing sandals.
c. favoring or advancing a particular point or view; partisan.
d. becoming young or youthful.

27. atlantean
a. covered with an armor, such as scales or bony plates.
b. having a soft voice.
c. of or relating to Atlas; having great strength.
d. arranged, occurring, or growing in pairs; twin.

28. feckless
a. lacking purpose or vitality; ineffective.
b. having the qualities of soap.
c. easily broken; breakable; fragile.
d. 1. marked by brutal or cruel crimes; vicious. 2. shamefully wicked; infamous.

29. stentorian
a. safeguarding against evil.
b. 1. given to the use of long words. 2. long and ponderous; polysyllabic.
c. extremely loud.
d. inclined to shed many tears; tearful.

30. cuckquean
a. the nape of the neck.
b. a female cuckold.
c. 1. a frenzied impassioned choric hymn and dance. 2. an irregular poetic expression suggestive of the ancient Greek dithyramb. 3. a wildly enthusiastic speech or piece of writing.
d. the amount of liquid by which a container falls short of being full.

31. hypergelast
a. a light blow made by pressing a fingertip against the thumb and releasing it.
b. a young animal, such as a lamb or calf, fattened for slaughter.
c. someone who never laughs.
d. someone who laughs excessively.

32. amanuensis

a. 1. an evil spirit that descends upon and has sexual intercourse with women as they sleep. 2. a nightmare or nightmarish burden.

b. a receptacle for keeping or displaying sacred relics.

c. a secretary.

d. 1. excrement; dung. 2. something morally offensive.

33. baronial

a. 1. of no value; worthless; trifling. 2. having no power, force, or effect.

b. 1. a stupid person. 2. a person afflicted with cretinism.

c. stately and grand.

d. 1. of, relating to, or characteristic of the Pharisees. 2. hypocritically self-righteous.

34. hebetudinous

a. making or given to noisy vehement outcry.

b. dull-minded; mentally lethargic.

c. 1. of or relating to a sepulcher. 2. suggestive of the grave; funereal.

d. 1. of or like twilight; dim. 2. becoming active at twilight.

35. caterwaul

a. 1. to walk through, over, or around. 2 to inspect an area on foot.

b. to reason methodically and logically.

c. 1. to give a thrashing to; beat. 2. to scold sharply; berate.

d. 1. to cry like a cat in heat. 2. to make a shrill, discordant sound. 3. to have a noisy argument.

36. boeotian

a. 1. of or relating to Cambridge, England, or Cambridge, Massachusetts. 2. of or relating to Cambridge University.

b. excessively or irrationally dutiful or devoted to one's wife.

c. 1. of, affected with, or resembling scrofula. 2. morally degenerate; corrupt.

d. dull; stupid.

37. cacology

a. 1. bad choice of words. 2. unacceptable pronunciation.

b. 1. bad handwriting. 2. incorrect spelling.

c. lack of concern; indifference.

d. a group of pundits who wield political influence.

38. obstreperous
a. producing warmth; heating.
b. having or furnished with teeth.
c. noisily defiant; unruly.
d. antismoke; antismoking.

39. chapfallen
a. of, relating to, or occurring in the morning; early.
b. dejected or dispirited.
c. 1. causing or capable of causing fear. 2. fearful; timid.
d. of or relating to a rope or cord.

40. ananias
a. an expression characterized by conciseness and elegance.
b. an expedition or an advance, especially a military one.
c. abnormal smallness of the head.
d. a habitual liar.

41. lubricious
a. relating to baths or bathing.
b. 1. having a slippery or smooth quality. 2. shifty or tricky. 3. lewd; wanton.
c. feeding on fish; subsisting on fish.
d. 1. having the temperament of one born under the astrological influence of Saturn. 2. melancholy or sullen.

42. malapert
a. 1. coming before; preceding. 2. expectant; anticipatory.
b. having a swarthy or black complexion and black hair.
c. thick-headed; dull; stupid.
d. impudently bold in speech or manner; saucy.

43. logolatry
a. veneration of words.
b. the science or study of words.
c. a person who knows only one language.
d. 1. the leader of a Greek chorus. 2. a leader or spokesperson.

44. xanthodontous
a. having yellow teeth.
b. 1. melancholy; morose. 2. having a peevish disposition.
c. having a background with a pattern of flowers and plants.
d. overlapping regularly and evenly, as roof tiles or fish scales.

45. fat-witted
a. fat and slovenly.
b. having or bearing a name; not anonymous.
c. 1. arrested in growth or development. 2. severely diminished.
d. thick-headed; stupid.

46. kakistocracy
a. abnormal fear of crowds.
b. government by the worst, least qualified citizens.
c. absolute dominion or jurisdiction; sovereignty.
d. slow painful urination.

47. fustigate
a. to free from a falsehood or misconception.
b. to make fruitful or productive.
c. 1. to declare false; deny. 2. to oppose.
d. 1. to punish harshly. 2. to criticize severely.

48. tergiversator
a. a woman regarded as scolding and vicious.
b. a person who knows only one language.
c. a renegade; an apostate.
d. 1. a petty unscrupulous lawyer. 2. one who quibbles over trivia.

49. collop
a. 1. the rarefied fluid running in the veins of gods. 2. a watery acrid discharge from a wound or ulcer.
b. 1. a slice of meat. 2. a fold of fat flesh.
c. 1. cerecloth. 2. a burial garment.
d. 1. a frenzy supposed to have been induced by nymphs. 2. an emotional frenzy.

50. factotum
a. a rooster.
b. 1. a ski trail packed with snow. 2. an unpaved trail or path, especially in mountainous terrain.
c. an assistant who serves in a wide range of capacities.
d. 1. dry food used as livestock feed. 2. food or provisions.

Answers to Quiz 2
26. d 27. c 28. a 29. c 30. b
31. d 32. c 33. c 34. b 35. d
36. d 37. a 38. c 39. b 40. d
41. b 42. d 43. a 44. a 45. d
46. b 47. d 48. c 49. b 50. c

Quiz 3

51. atrabilious
a. inducing or facilitating child-birth.
b. happening by accident or chance.
c. 1. melancholy; morose. 2. having a peevish disposition; surly.
d. highly intricate; extremely difficult to solve.

52. uberous
a. not cultured; coarse.
b. copious; plentiful; abundant; overflowing; fruitful.
c. cut or split easily.
d. kidney-shaped.

53. wheyface
a. seriousness, as in demeanor or treatment.
b. a man or woman who marries late in life.
c. an ant.
d. a person with a pallid face.

54. imbroglio
a. a confusing or complicated situation.
b. 1. cohabitating without legal marriage. 2. the state of being a concubine.
c. an irresistible urge or compulsion; a pernicious habit.
d. an imaginary place or state in which the condition of life is extremely bad.

55. steatopygia
a. 1. nature as a source of growth or change. 2. something that grows or changes.
b. the study of flags.
c. an excessive accumulation of fat on the buttocks.
d. overbearing pride or presumption; arrogance.

56. muliebrity
a. 1. a list of people who have died. 2. an obituary.
b. the condition of being a woman.
c. the science of language; comparative philology.
d. a dispute about words.

57. troglodyte
a. 1. a street urchin. 2. a person of the lowest class.
b. 1. a prehistoric cave dweller. 2. a person likened to a caveman.
c. 1. a heroic champion. 2. a strong supporter or defender of a cause.
d. 1. a self-important person. 2. a powerful, pompous person.

58. lugubrious
a. 1. of or containing a mixture of vernacular words with Latin words. 2. of or involving a mixture of two or more languages.
b. 1. of or relating to the spleen. 2. marked by bad temper or irritability.
c. mournful or doleful, especially to a ludicrous degree.
d. favoring or advancing a particular point or view; partisan.

59. florilegium
a. 1. a voluptuous, alluring woman. 2. one of the beautiful virgins of the Koranic paradise.
b. 1. laborious or intensive study. 2. something produced by laborious study or effort.
c. a small diacritic mark, such as an accent or a vowel mark.
d. 1. an anthology. 2. a collection of flowers.

60. meacock
a. an effeminate man; a hen-pecked husband.
b. a period of five years.
c. a woman's small handbag.
d. cosmetic or theatrical makeup.

61. redoubtable
a. full-figured; rounded; voluptuous.
b. making or given to noisy, loud, or vehement outcry.
c. 1. arousing fear; formidable. 2. commanding respect.
d. of a menacing or threatening nature; minacious.

62. minion
a. 1. a servile follower. 2. a minor official. 3. a person who is highly favored.
b. 1. a library or reading room. 2. a literary or scientific club.
c. 1. a learned person; a scholar. 2. an idiot savant.
d. 1. government by women. 2. a society ruled by women.

63. skullduggery
a. 1. personal allusions or references. 2. personal belongings or affairs.
b. trickery; unscrupulous behavior.
c. an abnormal fear of pain.
d. a monument honoring a dead person whose remains lie elsewhere.

64. edentulous
a. feeding on excrement.
b. toothless.
c. cheerful; merry; light-hearted.
d. warlike in manner or temperament; pugnacious.

65. omphalos
a. a state, region, or group that has predominant influence over others.
b. one who subjects oneself or others to flogging.
c. a fellowship or association.
d. 1. the navel. 2. the central part or focal point.

66. obtund
a. to talk casually; chat.
b. to journey or travel from place to place, especially, on foot.
c. 1. to make brown or dusky. 2. to darken.
d. to dull or deaden; to make less intense.

67. bumbledom
a. a downward slope.
b. an eleven-sided polygon.
c. the domain of incompetent bureaucrats.
d. littleness of mind; meanness.

68. louche
a. morally dubious; decadent.
b. fascinated by words.
c. of, relating to, or possessing intellectual or spiritual knowledge.
d. 1. bearing numerous leaves; leafy. 2. of, relating to, or resembling a leaf.

69. witling
a. a young person, animal, or plant.
b. 1. a would-be wit. 2. a person of scant wit.
c. 1. the period during which one is legally underage. 2. a period of immaturity.
d. the study of oneself.

70. uxorious
a. excessively mournful or doleful.
b. 1. of or relating to a sepulcher. 2. funereal.
c. excessively submissive to one's wife.
d. shaped like a tongue.

71. caliginous
a. moving or jumping from one thing to another; disconnected.
b. 1. resembling ashes. 2. of a gray color tinged with black.
c. dark and gloomy.
d. perching or adapted for perching.

72. dyspeptic

a. 1. having indigestion. 2. having a morose disposition.

b. 1. of or like an old woman. 2. senile.

c. 1. relating to or resembling a turtle or tortoise. 2. slow-moving, like a turtle.

d. impossible to break; indestructible.

73. sinecure

a. 1. a lingua franca. 2. a dialect that becomes the standard language over a larger area.

b. a position that requires little or no work but provides a salary.

c. the calling down of evil or a curse on someone.

d. petty bureaucracy; fussiness and stupidity of minor officials.

74. myriadigamous

a. containing lead.

b. abusive; foul-mouthed; scurrilous.

c. containing or of the nature of feces; fecal; polluted with filth.

d. pertaining to someone who marries all kinds.

75. subfusc

a. using or marked by the use of few words; terse or concise.

b. dark or drab; dingy.

c. having projections resembling the teeth of a comb.

d. relating to medicine or a physician.

Answers to Quiz 3

51. c 52. b 53. d 54. a 55. c
56. b 57. b 58. c 59. d 60. a
61. c 62. a 63. b 64. b 65. d
66. d 67. c 68. a 69. b 70. c
71. c 72. a 73. b 74. d 75. b

Quiz 4

76. a person who makes a display of his wealth or position
a. virago
b. plutogogue
c. vulgarian
d. mammon

77. to darken or obscure partially; to give a sketchy outline of
a. adumbrate
b. omphalous
c. omnibus
d. imbricate

78. strictly and inflexibly just
a. draconic
b. elephantine
c. rhadamanthine
d. laconic

79. to disembowel; to remove an essential part of something
a. deracinate
b. etiolate
c. extirpate
d. eviscerate

80. given to weeping; causing tears
a. lugubrious
b. lachrymose
c. lacrimal
d. bibulous

81. having broad buttocks
a. fat-witted
b. calipygous
c. platypygous
d. steatopygous

82. carnivorous; feeding on flesh
a. sarcophagous
b. ossivorous
c. ichthyophagous
d. granivorous

83. marked by irritability
a. banausic
b. vexillologic
c. scatologic
d. splenetic

84. indifferent or lukewarm
a. botryoidal
b. lubricious
c. laodicean
d. rhomboidal

85. relating to the pain and agony of death
a. antithalian
b. funereal
c. agonal
d. agonistes

86. lacking in nutrition; uninteresting; lacking maturity
a. jejune
b. junoesque
c. sapid
d. sipid

87. an effeminate man or boy
a. poltroon
b. braggadocio
c. minion
d. mollycoddle

88. fawning; characterized by
servile compliance
a. obloquial
b. obsequious
c. abstemious
d. futilitarian

89. one who makes a living
collecting refuse
a. ragamuffin
b. ragpicker
c. ruffian
d. tatterdemalion

90. to upset or discompose
a. untune
b. deliquesce
c. plume
d. untone

91. a wine-loving, riotous
reveler
a. careener
b. crooner
c. bacchant
d. teetotaler

92. characteristic of a hedgehog
a. erinaceous
b. ursine
c. porcine
d. pertinacious

93. fish eating
a. entomophagous
b. creophagous
c. rhizophagous
d. ichthyophagous

94. a person excessively
concerned with his or her
health
a. valetudinarian
b. invalid
c. malingerer
d. malapert

95. given to or expressing lust;
salacious
a. bumptious
b. caliginous
c. lascivious
d. perspicacious

96. infernal; relating to the
underworld
a. luciferous
b. chthonic
c. hellbent
d. hellacious

97. dung eating
a. sarcophagous
b. merdivorous
c. omnivorous
d. panivorous

98. delicate or translucent; insubstantial

a. unctuous
b. susurrus
c. diaphanous
d. diatonic

99. unspeakably horrible

a. atrabilious
b. abdominous
c. edentulous
d. infandous

100. mechanical; utilitarian

a. hebetudinous
b. banausic
c. anacusic
d. utile

Answers to Quiz 4

76. c 77. a 78. c 79. d 80. b
81. c 82. a 83. d 84. c 85. c
86. a 87. d 88. b 89. b 90. a
91. c 92. a 93. d 94. a 95. c
96. b 97. b 98. c 99. d 100. b

Quiz 5

101. obsessive use of obscene language
a. echolalia
b. glossolalia
c. coprolalia
d. coprolagnia

102. a small spherical mass
a. ort
b. globule
c. orb
d. ordure

103. sexless; effeminate
a. incondite
b. uxorious
c. epicene
d. uxorial

104. a trinket; a showy, cheap ornament
a. tule
b. bauble
c. globule
d. bomblet

105. villainous, wicked
a. plurifarious
b. octofarious
c. bifarious
d. nefarious

106. insincere or specious; attractive in a vulgar way
a. merdivorous
b. meretricious
c. mucilaginous
d. myriadigamous

107. a lover
a. paramour
b. louche
c. ananias
d. patois

108. corrosive; bitingly sarcastic
a. byzantine
b. coruscant
c. caustic
d. acoustic

109. to have extramarital affairs with woman
a. filander
b. assignat
c. pander
d. philander

110. a soft, whispering sound
a. wittol
b. susurrus
c. cicatrix
d. suppuration

111. last night
a. sennight
b. benighting
c. forenight
d. yesternight

112. cheerful eagerness or
willingness
a. zester
b. alacrity
c. acridity
d. celery

113. a scolding, ill-tempered
woman; a strong, courageous
woman
a. tarantass
b. taggant
c. vulgarian
d. virago

114. poorly constructed; crude
a. incondite
b. condign
c. inconic
d. condite

115. someone whose remarks or
writing is habitually banal
a. babylonian
b. succedaneum
c. platitudinarian
d. valetudinarian

116. lithe; agile
a. loathsome
b. lissome
c. noisome
d. woesome

117. the study of excrement;
obscene language or literature
a. scatology
b. cacology
c. abiology
d. psephology

118. harsh criticism; a
censorious remark
a. aversion
b. adversion
c. animadversion
d. anima

119. shining in the night
a. noctilucous
b. noctambulist
c. noctidiurnal
d. noctiferous

120. a regional dialect; the
characteristic jargon of a group
a. zygal
b. patois
c. frippery
d. argon

121. to weaken by arresting the
development of
a. gormandize
b. eviscerate
c. etiolate
d. etymologize

122. abhorrent; disgusting
a. boeotian
b. apollonian
c. loathsome
d. lissome

123. offensively assertive; pushy
a. bibulous
b. bumptious
c. bulbous
d. boisterous

124. dark or dusky; sooty

a. fuliginous
b. florilegium
c. uliginous
d. igneous

125. a scar

a. clerestory
b. cicada
c. clerisy
d. cicatrix

Answers to Quiz 5

101. c 102. b 103. c 104. b 105. d
106. b 107. a 108. c 109. d 110. b
111. d 112. b 113. d 114. a 115. c
116. b 117. a 118. c 119. a 120. b
121. c 122. c 123. b 124. a 125. d

Quiz 6

126. a person with mediocre talents
a. misandrist
b. misogynist
c. mediocrist
d. misoneist

127. being against laughter and enjoyment
a. antitheistic
b. antithetic
c. antithenar
d. antithalian

128. to pee
a. fulminate
b. expectorate
c. micturate
d. nictitate

129. characterized by insincere earnestness; oily
a. anfractuous
b. unctuous
c. erinaceous
d. obsequious

130. calumny; disgrace from public vilification
a. obloquy
b. colloquy
c. soliloquy
d. dentiloquy

131. the tinkling sound of bells
a. tinniness
b. tinnitus
c. tintinnabulation
d. ablution

132. H shaped
a. otiose
b. zygal
c. sphenoid
d. oviform

133. something that eases grief or pain
a. amanuensis
b. griever
c. absinthe
d. nepenthe

134. devious or scheming; intricate
a. schematic
b. byzaanchy
c. byzantine
d. benighted

135. niggardly, stingy
a. parsimonious
b. pediculous
c. simoniacal
d. diaphanous

136. dedicated to pleasure
a. acephalous
b. apolaustic
c. apotropaic
d. apolegamic

137. hardheartedness; unfeeling
a. kakistocracy
b. callosity
c. cellulosity
d. chirocracy

138. a ragamuffin
a. tatterdemalion
b. anthelion
c. pommelion
d. ragamala

139. one who observes or recommends silence
a. cotquean
b. quietus
c. silentiary
d. cuckquean

140. love of women
a. philocaly
b. philistine
c. philippic
d. philogyny

141. having a stately bearing; regal
a. atlantean
b. tartarean
c. junoesque
d. bunyanesque

142. having great beauty
a. platypygous
b. pulchritudinous
c. callipygous
d. calligraphic

143. to eat ravenously
a. deamidize
b. iridize
c. gormandize
d. iodize

144. lazy or indolent; useless; futile
a. epicene
b. redoubtable
c. chthonic
d. otiose

145. to verbally attack or denounce; to explode
a. farcinate
b. fulminate
c. fumigate
d. festinate

146. someone who favors the wealthy
a. plutogogue
b. factotum
c. troglodyte
d. silentiary

147. sorcery, witchcraft
a. rodomontade
b. collop
c. necromancy
d. tintinnabulation

148. the literati; the
intelligentsia
a. literalizer
b. clerisy
c. quincunx
d. quinary

149. lack of concern
a. chapfallen
b. insouciance
c. subfusc
d. banausic

150. intended to prevent bad
luck or evil
a. agonal
b. dyspeptic
c. apotropaic
d. apolaustic

Rejected Best Words

As I write on *The Vocabula Review*'s "Best Words" webpage, "Love a word? Tell us what it is and perhaps we'll add it to our list of The Best Words." I say "perhaps," because many of the words that people nominated as best words, I consider lackluster or worse. Here are some of the words that I rejected as best words.

Segue—which obviously belongs in a Worst Words list

Drismal—occasionally useful but hardly worthy of the "Best" designation

Food—among the starving, perhaps so; otherwise, no

Leet—slang for "good" or "great," apparently, and idiotic, certainly

procrastinate—which has nothing whatever, neither meaning nor music, to recommend it; only a procrastinator could love *procrastinate*

C.H.O.G.M.—"Commonwealth Heads Of Government Meeting," or CHO-gum. "I know, it's an acronym, but say it. Go on, it's the most fun word to say. I nearly named my first born CHOGM. CHOGM, CHOGM, CHOGM"

Constantinople—proper names are no more welcome than acronyms, "cool to say" though *Constantinople* may be

Cuntiferous—swear words and scatology belong in a Worst of the Worst Words list; only people as offensive, as humorless, as this word would ever use it

Diarrhea—or "diharrea," as the nominator spells it, does not, as he maintains, "sound pretty"

and/or—whether you believe this expression is useful or distasteful, in no circumstances is it a Best Word *putz* and *schmuck*—derivations aside, both words are insulting, mean-spirited, and slangy

floccinaucinihilipilification— though, as its nominator says, this is supposedly the longest word in the English language, it has nothing else—scarcely even its length—to support its being a Best Word

fracas—too dreadfully common to be justly regarded as a Best Word

cafeteria—no one who has eaten in a cafeteria could possibly consider this a Best Word

metamorphis—*metamorphosis* is certainly a good word, perhaps even a Best Word, but *metamorphis*, as the nominator spells it, is not

chocolate—taste, some people have yet to learn, differs from sound or sense

freal—"meaning, 'for real'; it sounds strange, but I like it," the nominator strangely writes

Index of Words

Acknowledgments

The definitions of the best words I have taken from a half dozen dictionaries. I have, in almost all instances, altered the wording though never, I trust, the meaning of these words.

The quotations that illustrate the use of the defined words I have largely culled from Google Books and my own library.

The principal source for the information in the "boxed" items is Wikipedia, though I have also consulted other sources. These paragraphs I have distilled from longer explanations.

Also from Robert Hartwell Fiske

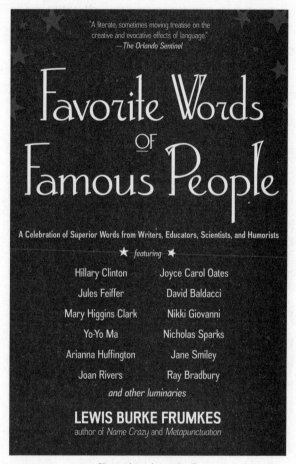